WHAT LEADERS ARE

BOOK 1 OF THE UNDERSTANDING LEADERSHIP SERIES

NATHAN NEBLETT

LUCIDBOOKS

What Leaders Are
Book 1 of the Understanding Leadership series

Copyright © 2018 by Nathan Neblett

Published by Lucid Books in Houston, TX
www.LucidBooksPublishing.com

ISBN-10: 1-63296-206-3
ISBN-13: 978-1-63296-206-5
eISBN-10: 1-63296-207-1
eISBN-13: 978-1-63296-207-2

Special Sales: Most Lucid Books titles are available in special quantity discounts. Custom imprinting or excerpting can also be done to fit special needs. Contact Lucid Books at Info@LucidBooksPublishing.com.

Table of Contents

Foreword	vii
Introduction	1
Chapter 1 – Leadership	5
Chapter 2 – Traits	13
Chapter 3 – Presence	23
Chapter 4 – Articulate	35
Chapter 5 – Compassionate	49
Chapter 6 – Service-minded	57
Chapter 7 – Intelligent	65
Chapter 8 – Enthusiastic	75
Chapter 9 – Visionary	83
Chapter 10 – Decisive	93
Chapter 11 – Persistent	103
Chapter 12 – Courageous	111
Conclusion	123
Appendix	127
Acknowledgments	147

Foreword

The more things change, the more they stay the same. As much as the internet, handheld devices, and other technology have affected our lives, one common denominator remains: the need for leadership. People always have, and always will, seek leadership in their workplace, in their communities, and throughout their society. *What Leaders Are* is a tremendous tool and leadership guide for both civilians and military. Whether the reader is a young novice or a seasoned professional with years of experience, Nathan Neblett's insights are valuable for all. Many years ago, Aristotle wrote that if you know what target you are trying to shoot at, you have a much better chance of hitting it. Filtered through his past experiences and objective analysis, Nathan provides the ideal target point for the reader. This book is more than just a simple model for the reader to emulate. It is instead a straightforward yet comprehensive analysis to help the reader internalize what leaders truly are. While there is no set formula or checklist for leadership, this book provides an interactive dialogue that challenges readers to grow, evolve, and develop their own leadership style. While the challenges of the world become more complicated and complex, the insights from *What Leaders Are* will be valuable for years to come.

Colonel Mark H. Clingan
United States Marine Corps
Commanding Officer, The Basic School

Dear reader, it is a grave undertaking to write a book, especially is it so in writing a treatise on success and failure, as we have attempted to do in the work we hereby present you. It is a solemn thing to give advice. Experience teaches that no one thing will please everybody; that men's censures are as various as their palates; that some are as deeply in love with vice as others are with virtue. Shall I then make myself the subject of every opinion, wise or weak? Yes, I would rather hazard the censure of some than hinder the good of others.

H. A. Lewis, *Hidden Treasures:*
Or, Why Some Succeed While Others Fail

Introduction

Purpose, Assumptions, and Layout

Another Book about Leadership?

When this book was written, LinkedIn had 15 types of leadership that you could add to your profile. When LinkedIn asked me to "endorse other people in your network," nine of the first 10 sought an endorsement for leadership. Today, people are aware of the value of leadership and have a desire to be seen as a leader.

The only thing to which I feel I can most accurately compare leadership is nutrition. The two are very similar: we are all generally familiar with the topics, we experience them daily in some way, and the battle over best practices rages around us. Any of us could write a book on leadership borrowing from nutrition. Just imagine the following titles:

Vegan Leadership: Don't Be the Office Carnivore
Paleo Leadership: Caveman Simple
Sugar-Free Leadership: No More Processed Leadership
Detox Leadership: Removing Toxins from Your Workplace

Leadership and nutrition both have innumerable styles, tools, and methods. Fortunately for nutrition, every theory on diet is bounded by basic building blocks: carbohydrates, fats, proteins, minerals, vitamins, and water. Knowing something about the basics can help everyone know which diets are acceptable and which ones may be unhealthy.

This book presents the building blocks of leadership. After reading this, you will have the antidote to ultra-modern versions of leadership, you'll be able to find the silver lining in the lessons you're offered, and you'll begin to see the true value in forging your own leadership product—yourself.

What Is the Purpose of This Book?

The first purpose of this book is to examine the concept of leadership, the difficulties associated with defining it, and the one truth beneath it all.

The second purpose of this book is to differentiate which parts of leadership are "need to know" and which ones are "nice to know." Some parts never change, and some parts do. How do you tell the difference? How do you evaluate the new material produced on this topic every day?

The third purpose of this book is to serve as a study guide to individuals and groups who want to actively pursue improvement in the "need to know" leadership abilities. If we can identify the building blocks of leadership, we can use them in leadership development programs, in MBA or other programs that aim to develop future leaders, and with individuals who are ready to take their next steps forward in self-development.

Background

This project began as the final project of a full-time MBA program. At the college, I conducted an online questionnaire to obtain current opinions on leadership and leaders. The questionnaire is included, along with the results, in the appendix to this book. Answers from the questionnaire are used throughout the text.

You can participate in the survey by filling it out in the appendix. NOTE: *If you did not participate in the survey, turn to the appendix and fill it in now.* That will help you understand many of the comments in the book since I refer to the survey throughout the text.

I made certain assumptions while writing this book:

1. Quotes from historic leaders are better understood in their original form, as are the survey responses. The literary excerpts included here may include potentially insensitive terminology or grammar that is not contemporary. For example, many authors and survey participants utilized only the masculine forms of pronouns when referring to unspecified individuals. Additionally, English was not the first language for all survey participants, and some errors exist, but original verbiage is included as much as possible to ensure that their chosen images are transmitted and not my interpretation of them.

2. You have seen someone in a leadership position. Whether at your job, at your school, at home, on your team, or on TV—at some point, you have worked with or for someone else or have been willing to work with or for someone else. That may have been a positive or a negative experience. Consider the following chart from the online survey. Just because we have seen leaders doesn't mean that we like them. When survey participants were asked to name a leader and state if they wanted to be like the person they named, here is how everyone responded.

Do you hope to be like the person you named as a leader?

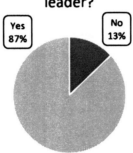

3. At some point, you have admired someone you have seen or read about, or you have admired a trait or quality in someone you have seen.

Layout

The chapters of this book are constructed in a similar format and contain the following parts:

- A word cloud that contains the key elements of that chapter's topic. Where data were available in the survey, the word cloud shows the distribution of the frequency of each answer—the bigger the word in the cloud, the more responses included that word. Following that is the definition of the chapter's key word as defined by *Merriam-Webster* online, accessed in June 2017. The bolded phrase is the definition I believe is most applicable to the chapter.
- Quotes from literature that support the topic.
  Are there timeless qualities of leadership within the writings of leaders from the distant past? The recent past? Or is leadership an evolving quality and all of its past forms transitory?

- Quotes from the questionnaire that support the topic.

  If we want to find consistent qualities in leadership, can you do that by comparing the past and the present? Comparing old and new opinions on the subject could reveal those critically consistent elements—the "need to know" about leadership.

- Food for thought, or exercises for you to know yourself and the subject better. (NOTE: Food for thought related to chapter 1 is presented in the conclusion.)

  - It would be easy to read a text or a few extracts from literature about this subject and move on. Undoubtedly, reading a book on leadership is a step forward, however small. A bigger step would be to reflect on what you read, determine which parts of it are most necessary for you, and begin practicing those skills today. The Food for Thought section gives you something to think about to further your study of the topic presented in each chapter—something to read, something to listen to, or something to do. It does no good to nod your head and silently agree as you read key thoughts unless you also have some way to incorporate new ideas and make them part of your toolkit. Practice makes perfect. Repetition is a key to learning.

Chapter 1

Leadership

noun lead·er·ship \'lē-dər-ˌship\

1

: the office or position of a leader • recently assumed the leadership of the company

2

: **capacity to lead** • a politician who lacks leadership

3

: the act or an instance of leading

• leadership molds individuals into a team—Harold Koontz & Cyril O'Donnell

4

: leaders • the party leadership

Everybody acknowledges a real leader—a man who is fit to plan and command. And when you find a real leader who bears a title, you will have to inquire of someone else what his title is. He doesn't boast about it.

A man may, by his industry, deserve advancement, but it cannot be possibly given him unless he also has a certain element of leadership. This is not a dream world we are living in.[1]

—Henry Ford, an industrialist, businessman,
inventor, and founder of the Ford Motor Company

How Do You Define Leadership?

The dictionary definition of leadership is brief and unsatisfying. If it were sufficient, I expect that many of the answers submitted in the questionnaire would have been similar to what is in the dictionary, or even identical. They are not. More than 500 unique definitions of leadership were offered by the participants in the questionnaire. While some words were used repeatedly, there was no clear winner on what leadership is. Other survey results indicated that defining leadership is difficult. Some participants believed that leadership could not be learned.

Is leadership something that you are born with, or something you can learn?

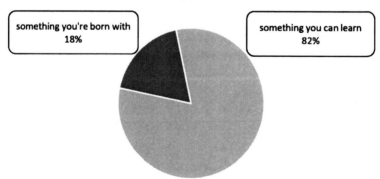

something you're born with
18%

something you can learn
82%

There was even more polarization when participants were asked to choose whether leadership is a trait or a verb.

In your opinion, is leadership a quality you have or something you do?

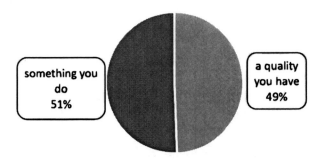

something you do 51%

a quality you have 49%

More than 180 participants selected a head of state when asked to name a leader. Fifty more selected CEOs, 47 selected social movement leaders, and 32 selected religious figures. Teachers, parents, team captains, military leaders, coaches, a blogger, a nail technician, and a video game character also made the list.

The word that appeared most often in the definition of leadership, the traits of a leader, and the actions that leaders take was some form of the word *inspire*. While that word was the most frequently used, many other words were submitted that were notably different: *tenacious, forthright, famous.*

Trying to put leadership into words is difficult. Trying to find people who agree about the definition of leadership is even more difficult. Not all 500 definitions are listed here, but the quotations below are representative of the variety. Some words occur more frequently than others and some are unique. Some definitions were lists of qualities, others were lists of actions, and some included both.

Define leadership by finishing the following sentence: "A leader is . . ."

- someone who has self-knowledge, intelligence and human sense
- someone who is enlightened, spiritual and humble
- strategic, people oriented, and trustable

- the hardest worker in the room, who is very modest and aspirational
- trustworthy, inspirational, and focused on developing the team
- bullish, controlling, and self-centered
- someone who drives forward individuals with like-minded goals
- a person who inspires and helps the others in his or her team to succeed in their duties
- a person who sets the goals and provides the tools for success for his team
- a servant, supporting and empowering those who work for her/him
- one who makes things happen, where others have failed
- one who shows the right path and encourages to follow it
- managing, directing, and controlling the project / program / business operations ERP IT goals / KPIs of the process and systems; being transparent to all business staff / units having open, honest, direct conversations. With a keen eye on the profits-cost factors.

The questionnaire revealed significant differences of opinion about the definition of a leader, but one thing is certain: **We know one when we see one.**

Henry Ford wrote, "Everybody acknowledges a real leader."[2] Each of us knows whom we would and would not follow. Each of us can name people whom we consider to be leaders and others we wouldn't follow even out of simple curiosity. We may disagree with everyone else's list, in part or in whole. Look at the list of leaders named in the appendix. How many of the leaders do you not know?

Many books and articles offer a view of leadership from the leader's perspective, but look at it from the other side, from the ones who must choose or follow a leader. In a survey with more than 500 respondents, there were 239 people named as a leader and more than 170 traits used to describe them. For those people named most frequently, participants chose different traits that they admired about the same person.

Leadership Looks Different to Different People

The concept of leadership is different for nearly every person. That is part of what makes leadership so difficult to define. Each author of a book or article adds to the list of people named as a leader or to the list of leadership traits. The survey included here could be seen as more than 500 separate articles telling us what leadership looks like and what its key factors are. Despite the endless possibilities that this implies, the single truth remains that everybody thinks of *someone* as a real leader.

Added to this is the fact that people learn by observation and emulation. If we see someone we admire, we may mimic them in order to learn. Children learn this way, and so do adults. Now imagine the list of leaders that you would name. If you were to emulate them and apply their leadership styles to your situation, the final product would be the combination of the leaders you emulated and your firsthand experiences. These would combine to give you a unique understanding and a unique outlook as a leader. Now try to define leadership. The definition is nebulous because we are all looking at something different, and we have all had different experiences. We all choose to follow different people at different times and for different reasons. When we assume a position in which we are leading others, we become a mix of what we have seen in our leaders and what we have learned along our life's journey. That makes us different from others in leadership positions.

Each of us becomes a unique leader. We each face unique problems, and we face them with different teams of people.

Julius Caesar conquered Gaul. Mahatma Gandhi united India and led its citizens to independence. Julius Caesar may not have been able to unite India, and Mahatma Gandhi may not have been able to conquer the Gauls. Still, they were both the optimal leader for where they were and when they led. Here is the real question about leadership: What do you need to be and what do you need to do to become the leader that people around you need right now? **Leadership isn't defined by what you think of yourself. Leadership is defined by what others think of you and what you can accomplish together.** As situations change and the makeup of each group of people changes, the characteristics of the leader they seek are also changing, which is why one survey participant named a sports star as a leader and another named a revolutionary.

The opportunity that this knowledge provides is that you can be the leader that *someone* is looking for. Despite the fluid definitions of leadership and the hundreds of people named as leaders, there are constants. This book and its sequel are dedicated to looking at leaders through the centuries, comparing them to opinions gathered today and examining two things about leaders that are constants:

- What leaders are
- What leaders do

Leadership is a trait that is made up of other traits; it is an action that is the sum of daily actions.

Because people have traits in differing quantities, their leadership looks different than those around them. Let this encourage you. That means that *no one* has the perfect recipe for leadership. *No one* can tell you that you are not a leader or that you have no leadership abilities. You just have a different type and a different amount. You can focus on these building blocks and develop your leadership ability over time to be ever-ready for the next opportunity.

Become the leader that people need, where you are, right now.

Why Isn't That Happening Already?

But, although provided with these instruments of war, if the leader be not competent, a brooding hen might as well strike a badger, or a dog with young challenge the tiger: the spirit of encounter may be present, but there is no end but death.[3]

—*Wu Ch'i (also known as Wutzu), a successful strategist and general in China who lived around 400 BC*

We sometimes imagine a leader rising up on his or her natural talent to take their place at the top of an organization or at the front of a group. What happens more often is that someone is selected to a leadership position based on seniority within an organization, a connection with someone in authority, or a vote of popularity (particularly in clubs and similar organizations). If you've ever worked for someone like that, you know who really cares about the key ingredients of leadership—you. Understanding the perspective of those who follow the leader matters.

What if you are lifted to a position of leadership? If you want to excel and take pride in your role, you could try to learn all the lessons the old-fashioned way—at the school of hard knocks, learning from your mistakes—or you could begin to study leadership and make a difference for others today. What do you study? Of the nearly infinite number of articles and books available, which one is right? Or more accurately, which one is right for *you*? Returning to the definitions collected in the survey, which one will you strive to be?

- a person others look up to, and wish to follow or emulate
- a superwoman
- confident, but humble
- curious, passionate, and determined
- fair and unambiguous
- helpful and intelligent
- powerful and dominant

and/or

- somebody who knows the way, shows the way and goes the way
- someone that makes me want to be better
- someone that we can trust
- someone who can take responsibility
- someone who has a vision and able to convince people to follow him/her
- someone who inspires others and is able to influence people
- someone who makes everyone feel equal and important

Each new article or book you read offers you a chance to critically consider whether you are reading about an unchanging principle of leadership or a principle that is specific in time, specific to one group of people, or specific to one situation. Your ability to tell the difference will be helpful as you grow into your own form of leadership.

References

1. Henry Ford, *My Life and Work* (Garden City, NY: Doubleday, Page & Co., 1923), 76.

2. Ibid.

3. Sunzi and Wutzu, *The Book of War: The Military Classic of the Far East*, trans. Captain E. F. Calthrop, R.F.A. (London, John Murray, 1908), 76.

Chapter 2

Traits

noun \ˈtrāt, British usually ˈtrā\

1

a : a distinguishing quality (as of personal character)

b : an inherited characteristic

2

a : a stroke of or as if of a pencil

b : touch, trace

From the Literature

Pick out or underline the leadership traits listed in the following excerpts from literature and compare what you found to the table below.

The Master replied: The wise and good ruler is benevolent without expending treasure; he lays burdens on the people without causing them to grumble; he has desires without being covetous; he is serene without being proud; he is awe-inspiring without being ferocious. . . . In imposing burdens, he chooses the right time and the right means, and nobody can grumble. His desire is for goodness, and he achieves it; how should he be covetous? The wise and good ruler never allows himself to be negligent, whether he is dealing with many men or with few, with small matters or with great. Is this not serenity without pride? He has his cap and robe properly adjusted, and throws a noble dignity into his looks, so that his gravity inspires onlookers with respect. Is he not thus awe-inspiring without being ferocious?[1]

—Confucius wrote his philosophy in approximately 500 BC
A significant portion of Asia continues to employ the philosophy of Confucius
as part of their practices of governance

Wu the Master said:—

"The leader of the army is one who is master of both arms and letters. He who is both brave and tender can be entrusted with troops.

"In the popular estimation of generals, courage alone is regarded; nevertheless, courage is but one of the qualifications of the leader. Courage is heedless in encounter; and rash encounter, which is ignorant of the consequences, cannot be called good.

"There are five matters which leaders must carefully consider.

"First, reason; second, preparation; third, determination; fourth, vigilance; fifth, simplicity.[2]

—Wu Ch'i (also known as Wutzu)

His sagacity, intellectual force, versatility, originality, firmness, fortunate period of service, and longevity combined to make him a great leader of his people. In American public affairs the generation of wise leaders next to his own felt for him high admiration and respect; and the strong republic, whose birth and youthful growth he witnessed, will carry down his fame as political philosopher, patriot, and apostle of liberty through long generations.[3]

—*Charles W. Eliot writing about Benjamin Franklin*

Each officer must endeavor by all means in his power to develop within himself those qualities of leadership, including industry, justice, self-control, unselfishness, honor, and courage, which will fit him to be a real leader.[4]

—*Major General John A. Lejeune,*
13th Commandant of the United States Marine Corps

The Qualities You Have

The search to understand the qualities that work together to define leadership began several thousand years ago, but it hasn't ended. Put the word *leadership* into an internet search engine. I did, and I received "about 809 million results." Scrolling through some of them, I found lists of traits, qualities, essentials, and so on. In the online survey, 500 participants listed a total of 172 traits when asked this question:

For the person you named, what one trait do you believe most strongly contributes to your opinion of them as a leader? Please use one word to complete the following sentence: "He or she is very _____."

The answers are all listed in the appendix. They were also used to form the word cloud at the beginning of the chapter.

Many people in the survey also defined leadership with a list of traits. A leader is:

- reliable, responsible, knowledgeable, relatable, realistic, and a self-starter
- somebody who is conscientious, courageous and caring
- someone who is strong, relatable, and caring
- someone kind, open minded, and respectful
- trustworthy, consistent

Here is a brief comparison of the qualities of a leader from the quoted extracts above and the survey's top 10:

Confucius	Wu Tzu	Elliot (on Franklin)	Maj Gen Lejeune	Survey Top 10
Wise	Master of both arms and letters	Sagacity	Industry	Inspirational
Good	Brave	Intellectual force	Justice	Charismatic
Benevolent	Tender	Versatility	Self-control	Visionary
Imposing	Courage	Originality	Unselfishness	Humble
Desires good-ness	Reason	Firmness	Honor	Strong
Serene	Preparation	Fortunate period of service	Courage	Persistent
Awe-inspiring	Determination	Longevity		Compassionate
	Vigilance			Selfless
	Simplicity			Determined
				Courageous

There are more lists—many more—from centuries of literature. Some of the traits are consistent over time; some are not. We'll focus our study in this book on character traits, usually expressed in one word, as shown above. NOTE: There are traits listed that may be out of your control. For example, "fortunate period of service" is listed for Benjamin Franklin. None of us controls the time during which we live. Franklin lived at a time of intense change. Even though we can't control this, we can make every effort to be ready for our leadership opportunities when they come.

So which traits do we need to know and in what measure? How do we find the "need to know" and separate it from the "nice to know"? One person may not be able to dedicate his life to the study of hundreds of character traits in order to become the perfect leader. That would be a waste of time anyway. As soon as someone mastered the currently listed qualities, another desired quality would be added to the list by a new generation. Let's break the traits down and determine how to focus on the critical ones.

- A "need to know" trait is one that forms a key part of every leader's story. It is a quality that would be missed if you tried to lead without it. It is a quality that should be studied and practiced if you are taking on a leadership role.
- A "nice to know" trait contributes to a specific leadership situation but isn't equally universal. These traits could vary because of the industry you are in, the country in which you live, or the age of the people you are leading. For example, participants from France listed *charismatic* three times more than the second-most popular trait. Participants between the ages of 36 and 45 listed *humble* more than any other trait. Some traits are "nice to know" depending on what you are doing, where you are, and who you're with.

The difference is important to understand but requires that you understand how traits work.

How Do Traits Work?

Character traits have a discernible measure of quantity and quality. Consider this statement by President Barack Obama from a speech on climate change that he gave at Georgetown University on June 25, 2013:

"I don't have much patience for anyone who denies that this challenge is real."[5]

Clearly, there is a quantity of patience implied here. Furthermore, this statement implies that the quantity of patience can change depending on the subject being discussed.

Someone can be more intelligent than someone else, stronger, more courageous, and so on. But with a change in quantity comes a change in quality. Consider again these words from Confucius: "The wise and good ruler is. . .awe-inspiring without being ferocious."[6] There is a limit to how much of a trait is good. The word *inspire* appeared more times among the open-ended responses of the survey than any other verb. It would seem that a leader who can inspire is very good. If so, to inspire more must surely be better. Confucius wisely pointed out that this is not the case when he wrote, "He has his cap and robe properly adjusted, and throws a noble dignity into his looks, so that his gravity inspires onlookers with respect. Is he not thus awe-inspiring without being ferocious?"[7]

The objective is to inspire awe and respect through his appearance, "without being ferocious," or overdoing it.

Consider a trait depicted like this:

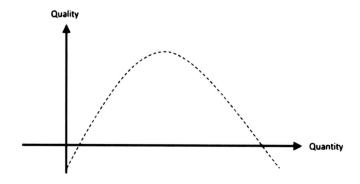

Having none of the trait adds zero to your leadership and could even subtract value. There is some ideal amount. And then there is too much, which could also subtract value from your leadership efforts.

Warnings

Having none of a necessary quality is a defect. Too much of a good thing is spoiled by excess. We have all heard maxims about avoiding extremes. That same warning applies here. Aristotle was a Greek philosopher who lived in the fourth century BC and became the tutor of Alexander the Great. Look carefully at Aristotle's warning about courage:

> It is the same then with temperance, courage, and the other virtues. A person who avoids and is afraid of everything and faces nothing becomes a coward; a person who is not afraid of anything but is ready to face everything becomes foolhardy. Similarly he who enjoys every pleasure and never abstains from any pleasure is licentious; he who eschews all pleasures like a boor is an insensible sort of person. For temperance and courage are destroyed by excess and deficiency but preserved by the mean state.[8]

Let's start with Wu Ch'i's statement:

Be *courageous*, but not so courageous that you *act rashly*.

Now add Aristotle's observation about the opposite of excess, the defect (or absence of):

Don't be *a coward*. Be *courageous*, but not so courageous that you *act rashly*.

Finally, there is a warning in all of these writings about the limitations of traits. Sun Tzu wrote a book called *The Art of War*, a classic manual on strategy that is studied in leadership programs in both the military and business. Sun Tzu also listed faults a leader must avoid. Those traits must *not* make up part of a leader's character. Viewed in the manner described above, some of these are just traits taken to the extreme:

> Generals must be on their guard against these five dangerous faults: - Blind impetuosity, which leads to death. Over-cautiousness, which leads to capture. Quick temper, which brings insult. A too rigid propriety, which invites disgrace. Over-regard for the troops, which causes inconvenience.[9]

Impetuosity is the result of too much courage (acting rashly). Over-cautiousness is too much caution. A quick temper can be the result of being too just. Too rigid propriety is too much propriety. Over-regard for the troops is too much compassion, giving more importance to comfort than to the task at hand. Confucius named four things that a leader must completely avoid:

> What are the four evil things?- The Master said: Cruelty: - Leaving the people in their native ignorance, yet punishing their wrong-doing with death. Oppression: - requiring the immediate completion of tasks imposed without previous warning. Ruthlessness: - giving vague orders, and then insisting on punctual fulfillment. Peddling husbandry: - stinginess in conferring the proper rewards on deserving men.[10]

Whether we're discussing the "need to know" or you go on to study the "nice to know," make sure you understand where the extremes are and what the trait must avoid. For every trait you study, be able to state the limit and the extreme case. Let's continue the example above:

Don't be *a coward*. Be *courageous,* but not so courageous that you *act rashly.* And don't *be ignorant of the consequences.*

Each trait can be thought of in the same manner, with the same model used to contemplate the effects of having too much or too little.

What Do We "Need to Know"?

As you sift through lists in history or lists online today, you will find common threads that are part of every success story. Based on the survey and the literature by and about leaders throughout the centuries, you will see that critical traits fall into one of the following chapters, expressing what a leader is (or has, in the case of *presence*).

Food for Thought

Read this:

1. Sun Tzu's masterpiece on strategy, *The Art of War,* contains numerous lists of ingredients for success. They are written plainly, as plainly as the traits of a leader are listed here. There are numerous free online sources where you can read this work. Take a look at the writing style and the way he used lists to describe various things. Do you think this is an effective way to write down instructions? Which lists stand out as the most valuable for you? The most memorable?

2. Type "article on leadership" into an internet search engine. Select one article about leadership traits, characteristics, or qualities, and then read it. Do they fit into the categories explained in this chapter? Do you agree with the traits, characteristics, or qualities listed? Why or why not? Is the trait you put in the survey in the article?

Watch this:

1. Type "leadership traits" into a video search engine. Select a video on leadership qualities, traits, or characteristics and watch it. Do you agree? Does the trait you wrote in the survey make their list?

Do this:

1. Find one list in literature (or an online article) for traits of a leader. How many of the traits named there match the ones in the word cloud at the beginning of the chapter? Which ones are "need to know"? "Nice to know"?

2. For the traits in the article you read, write out the following to think about the limits and potential downside of the traits you found.

Don't be (_____). Be (*trait*), but not so (*trait*) that you (*consequence of too much trait*). And don't (*extreme consequence of trait*).

References

1. Confucius, *The Sayings of Confucius*, trans. Lionel Giles (London: John Murray, 1907), 50, 51.

2. Sunzi and Wutzu, 76.

3. Charles William Eliot, *Four American Leaders* (Boston: American Unitarian Association, 1906), 29–30.

4. United States Marine Corps, *Leading Marines* (Washington, DC: Marine Corps Publications Electronic Library, 2016), 2-2.

5. Barack Obama, "Remarks by the President on Climate Change," at Georgetown University on June 25, 2013 (Washington, DC: The White House), accessed January 11, 2018 at https://obamawhitehouse.archives.gov/the-press-office/2013/06/25/remarks-president-climate-change.

6. Confucius, 51.

7. Ibid.

8. Aristotle, "Nicomachean Ethics," p. 37-38, (New York, MacMillan & Co, 1892)

9. Sunzi and Wutzu, 46.

10. Confucius, 51.

Chapter 3

Presence

noun pres·ence \ˈpre-zən(t)s\

1

: the fact or condition of being present

2

a : the part of space within one's immediate vicinity

b : the neighborhood of one of superior especially royal rank

3

archaic : see company 2a

4

: one that is present: such as

a : the actual person or thing that is present

b : something present of a visible or concrete nature

5

a : the bearing, carriage, or air of a person; especially: stately or distinguished bearing

b : a noteworthy quality of poise and effectiveness • the actor's commanding presence

6

: something (such as a spirit) felt or believed to be present

What Is It?

There are moments when someone can appear, and just by being there, they inspire. Several people who took the survey viewed presence as a primary quality in leaders. A leader is:

- showing the example
- always balanced and calm
- always in control and aware
- a self-confident person
- an embodiment of the organizational ideal, a manifestation of its values, a strategic visionary who sees the way forward and inspires cohesion and action in the team through compassion and selfless service
- balanced

Many participants listed charisma as a key trait for leaders. Definitions for charisma often highlight someone's attractiveness or the ability to inspire personal loyalty. I have chosen to break charisma down into two of its facets: having presence and being articulate. For the purpose of this chapter, *presence* is defined as the effect you have on others which is achieved by everything except speech and specific action.

As people get to know you, your presence becomes the symbol of your reputation. Even if you say nothing, they know what you have done, what you stand for, and what you will probably do next. Over time, your presence is the symbol of yourself and your company or team.

Some people cause us to change our attitude just by coming into our day. "I'm glad she's here. Now we know this will get done on time." It may be that people come into your space who cause you to become defensive, who cause you to smile, or who give you a sense of relief. What effect do you have on others when you enter a room? More importantly, what effect do you want to have? Knowing this, you can begin to build your presence.

People in leadership positions are watched very closely by the people around them. That is because we trust what we see more than we trust what we hear. Anyone who has heard the phrase, "Move along, nothing to see here," knows that there *is* something to see. Words can be used to manipulate us, so we look at facial expressions, body movements, and other outward physical signs to know what is *really* going on. Your presence is a significant part of your leadership. It will be watched, and it will influence the people around you.

Strong . . . Slender . . . Frail

While presence is a "need to know" trait, there is no single answer as to how you should appear physically. A monk named Eginhard wrote a biography of Charlemagne, who was crowned emperor of the Romans and gave rise to the Holy Roman Empire. Eginhard described Charlemagne in the following manner:

> His body was large and strong; his stature tall but not ungainly, for the measure of his height was seven times the length of his own feet. The top of his head was round; his eyes were very large and piercing. His nose was rather larger than is usual; he had beautiful white hair; and his expression was brisk and cheerful; so that, whether sitting or standing, his appearance was dignified and impressive. Although his neck was rather thick and short and he was somewhat corpulent this was not noticed owing to the good proportions of the rest of his body.[1]

When you read this description of Charlemagne, what stands out? Do any parts of his physical description seem particularly admirable or attract attention?

During the Crimean War, a British nurse named Florence Nightingale achieved national fame for her service in the battlefield hospitals. Hamilton Wright Mabie and Kate Stephens found a description of her in the letters of patients and the books of historians:

> "As her slender form glided quietly along each corridor every poor fellow's face softens with gratitude at the sight of her," wrote another. . . . No one who has observed her fragile figure and delicate health can avoid misgivings lest these should fail. . . . "To see her pass was happiness," one poor fellow said. . . . "The magic of her power over men used often to be felt," wrote Kinglake the historian, "in the room—the dreaded, the blood-stained room—where 'operations' took place. There perhaps the maimed soldier, if not yet resigned to his fate,

might at first be craving death rather than meet the knife of the surgeon; but when such a one looked and saw that the honoured lady-in-chief was patiently standing by him and, with lips closely set and hands folded, decreeing herself to go through the pain of witnessing pain, he used to fall into the mood of obeying the silent command, and, finding strange support in her presence, bring himself to submit and endure."[2]

While the physical characteristics differ in each case, notice that they are very carefully captured by the authors. People are watching you and noting your build, the color of your hair, and other features about your body, as well as the way you move it—how you control it or don't control it. As you read the biographies of leaders, there is typically a point at which the author describes the person in detail to communicate to the reader what it was like to be in that person's presence. The most immediately visible part of your presence is the shape and posture of your body. The descriptions above are varied and demonstrate that different situations allow different adjectives to apply. "Fragile" was applied in the case of Florence Nightingale despite her strong ability to change a situation with only her presence. On the opposite end of the spectrum, Charlemagne was described as "somewhat corpulent." Notice the words that French Captain André Dubarle used to describe General Foch, Supreme Commander of the Allied troops during World War I:

> "General Foch," he reminds his parents, "is a former commander of the School of War, where he played, on account of his great fitness, a very remarkable role.
>
> "He is a man still young [he was almost 63!], slender and supple, and rather frail; his powerful head seems like a flower too heavy for a stem too slight.
>
> "What first strikes one about him is his clear gaze, penetrating, intellectual, but above all and in spite of his tremendous energy, luminous. This light in his eyes spiritualizes a countenance which otherwise would be brutal, with its big mustache bristling above a very prominent, dominant jaw."[3]

Frail may seem an atypical adjective for a military commander, especially compared to Charlemagne's corpulence. Just like the definition of leadership, there is wide variety in what a leader looks like.

While the differences between leaders may be great, there are some "nice to know" factors that will apply to your appearance, depending on where you are. For example, as a Marine officer, neither frail nor corpulent would have been considered acceptable descriptors. Marines typically prefer someone who is fit and demonstrates physical ability that will be useful when situations become difficult. In an office setting, that may be less important, although still admirable. Observe your situation carefully and your role in it before determining how you should appear, how to move, and what emotions to display. Simultaneously, observe the people you believe to be effective leaders and note what you believe to be their key physical attributes. Remember that your physical state overlaps with other critical leadership components such as the ability to persist. Being fit allows you to endure. It is up to you to observe and decide on the appearance you need. You can usually create the body you want through diet and exercise while choosing the appearance you want with things as simple as a haircut and a change of clothes. Your choices directly affect your appearance and the beginning of your presence.

The adjectives you choose to become will define your presence, but how you move will be equally important. One term for what you communicate through your movement is body language. Pericles ruled over the Greek empire during the Golden Age of peace in which art and culture flourished in that empire. Plutarch wrote about Pericles' attributes as follows:

> For [Anagoraxas], Pericles entertained an extraordinary esteem and admiration, and. . .derived hence not merely, as was natural, elevation of purpose and dignity of language, raised far above the base and dishonest buffooneries of mob eloquence, but, besides this, a composure of countenance, and a serenity and calmness in all his movements, which no occurrence whilst he was speaking could disturb.[4]

Pericles had admired these qualities—dignity of language, composure of countenance (face), serenity, calmness in all his movements—so much in another leader that he wanted to emulate them. Just like Pericles, if you admire qualities in someone else, you can emulate them. In this case, carefully note the descriptors of how Pericles moved—with serenity and calmness.

Take a moment to think of other descriptive words that can be applied to a person's movement. What can you list?

> Clumsy? Awkward? Goofy?
> Graceful? Strong? Confident?

There is a wide range of words you can put on your list. Typically, those in the word cloud and in the biographies of leaders throughout history are those that are critical parts of presence.

Finally, know that there are other "nice to know" qualities of movement, depending on your location. In Japan, body movements have specific meanings. In Korea, people observe your posture. Take note of these and other culturally relevant facets of your person and your movement when required.

Control Your Movements and Your Face

Consider the following recommendations from *George Washington's Rules of Civility*, written or copied when he was a teenager. In the rules, he wrote instructions for every moment of action in polite society. Here is an excerpt for what should and should not be displayed on your face:

> 19th let your Countenance be pleasant but in Serious Matters Somewhat grave. . . .

> The face should not look fantastic, changeable, absent, rapt in admiration, covered with sadness, various and volatile, and it should not show any signs of an unquiet mind. On the contrary, it should be open and tranquil, but not too expansive with joy in serious affairs, nor too self-contained by an affected gravity in the ordinary and familiar conversation of human life.[5]

Some of your facial features—eyes, nose, and so on—are naturally occurring and cannot be changed. But your expressions can be changed. George Washington's list of what *not* to do with your face is helpful in this regard. If you're not sure what you want to express, at least know that there are things that should not be expressed. His rules of civility include that and many more classical hints on posture, movement, and so forth.

What do you wish to communicate with your presence? Is it apparent on your face? Which of the adjectives in Washington's description do you typically display? Our expressions are usually a subconscious reaction, so give it careful attention. Notice what your face communicates. You have probably heard terms such as *active listening* in which you try to show that you are paying attention to another person. Looking at Washington's instructions, you can also practice active calm and avoid extremes or volatility of emotion. Paying attention to your facial expressions in conversation and being aware that you control them are the first steps to presenting the expressions you want.

"The Apparel Oft Proclaims the Man"

Clothing is mentioned frequently in biographies and stories. Clothes play a significant role in how a person is perceived. Confucius described the good and wise ruler: "He has his cap and robe properly adjusted, and throws a noble dignity into his looks, so that his gravity inspires onlookers with respect."[6] One of Shakespeare's characters in *Hamlet* also gives advice about wardrobe:

> Costly thy habit as thy purse can buy,
> But not express'd in fancy; rich, not gaudy;
> For the apparel oft proclaims the man.[7]

To be very clear, while one of Shakespeare's characters recommends spending as much as you can afford on your clothes, that is hyperbole and not necessary. You can take action with the clothes you have and change your appearance and your presence today. Again, consider George Washington's Rules of Civility:

> 51st Wear not your Cloths, foul, . . . or Dusty but See they be Brush'd once every day at least and take heed that you approach not to any Uncleanness. . . .
>
> Do not let your clothes be dirty, torn, covered with dust or threadbare. Have them brushed at least once a day. And take care also in what place you sit down, or kneel, or rest your elbows, that it be not unfit or filthy. Do not carry your cloak over your arm after the manner of swaggerers. And when you take off your coat or cloak, fold them neatly and carefully, and take care where you put them.
>
> 52nd In your Apparel be Modest and endeavour to accomodate Nature, rather than to procure Admiration keep to the Fashion of your equals Such as are Civil and orderly with respect to Times and Places.[8]

First, heed Washington's advice to dress in a way that is appropriate for your surroundings—"fashion of your equals such as are civil and orderly." Don't be overly fancy when unnecessary, and don't undershoot the mark, either. Overshooting the mark is pretentious. Undershooting the mark communicates that the people around you weren't worth the effort of dressing appropriately. As always, there can be too little or too much. When in doubt, if you have a meeting or are visiting somewhere you have never been, ask someone who knows. You can often call ahead to the meeting place or restaurant and ask what is normally worn. If it is not a situation in which you can call ahead, ask someone who has been there before. The goal is to be dressed to a level similar to those around you and appropriate to the situation. Your physical presence, your facial features, and your attention to detail will make you stand out, even when you are dressed like everyone else.

Ironing your clothes demonstrates that you care about details. Be sure to mend any tears or replace missing buttons. Clean your shoes. Shine your shoes if they are leather. Consider any slogans that are written on your shirts. Do they communicate what you want to communicate? There are schools of thought that encourage people to be unconcerned with these "mortal trappings," but that can appear as carelessness, which is rarely inspiring to a broader audience. Simple rules of cleanliness and order go a long way, whatever you are wearing. Like everything, you can go too far. George Washington also wrote, "Do not delight in strutting like a peacock, or look proudly around to see if you are well decked."[9] Not fancy, not gaudy, not strutting like a peacock, but a dignified look can inspire. Be clean, be correct, but no need to be too chic.

Remember that your presence can be either welcome or unwelcome. If you're not trying to offend or be otherwise repulsive, following simple hygiene practices demonstrates respect for those around you. Understand that different countries and cultures have different standards, but typically, if people can smell your presence, you should change your habits. Your body, your mouth, or your clothes may be a source of those issues. Recognizing the impact of the cleanliness of you and your clothes can set you up for a great start, whether making a first impression or working to establish your reputation.

Conclusion

You may have seen a salesperson who wore the logo of the company on his or her shirt when conducting business. In that case, that person was borrowing the reputation of the company in order to do the company's business. That salesperson was a piece of the company's image. His or her behavior and image were meant to reflect the company's practice.

When in a leadership role, the company or team image is a reflection of you. You don't always wear a logo because people already know who you are and they are watching to see the standards you set for yourself and those around you. Are the standards calm, cool, and collected or something else?

We've all heard the saying "fake it 'til you make it," but in the case of presence, people can detect a fake. Envision the presence you want to have and work toward it every day—appearance, movements, facial expressions, and apparel. Choose the phrase "practice makes perfect," because your image will be a lifetime pursuit. Small changes will add up over time. Be persistent. There is no need to obsess over appearance; just give it some attention. Research your situation, make a vision for what you want to look like, and get started. Following the example of Pericles and the advice of George Washington, you don't have to come up with new ideas right away. Imitate, then innovate. Follow the simple rules you see in those you admire. When you get comfortable, build your own distinct presence from there.

Don't be *unkempt*. Have *presence*, but not so much that *you become gaudy or seem ferocious*. And don't *strut like a peacock*.

Food for Thought

Read This:

1. *George Washington's Rules of Civility* may seem out of date, but it carefully considers the impact of every action you can take in public. It is an excellent study in how to actively think about your presence. While the modern application of some rules may be limited, there are many instructions in the rules that are of immediate utility.

2. Plutarch's *The Lives of the Noble Grecians and Romans* is one of the first known compilations of biographies. Choose one biography and read it. Plutarch spends some time describing each person's presence. For the person

you picked, how does his or her presence seem to you? Alternatively, read the biography of one of the Caesars written by Suetonius, who also dedicates a portion of each book to communicating the Caesar's presence. For the Caesar you selected, how is his presence described?

Watch This:

1. Find the video for a song by Superchick titled "Rock What You Got." Like other titles by the band, many of their songs are very observant about self-image and presence.

2. Search a video archive for "presence." Choose one and watch it. Do you agree with the speaker's version of presence?

3. What is your favorite movie? Who is your favorite character? How is the presence of that character portrayed, and does it make a difference? Remember, presence is how you inspire or influence without further words or actions. How does this character's appearance on screen affect others? Does it seem believable to you?

Do This:

1. Think of who has a great presence in your life—a co-worker, a parent, a coach. What gives them this presence? What external factors contribute to their image? Clothes? Cleanliness? Physical build? Like Pericles, what can you do to begin to mimic those factors?

2. Today, change one thing about your appearance to move toward the image and presence you desire. You can do that without spending any money. You can clean your clothes and shoes in the sink, you can iron your clothes (borrow an iron, if necessary), you can comb your hair, wash your face, and brush your teeth. Start becoming today the person you want to be tomorrow and develop your presence. It is a step-by-step process, so take the first step and stick to it.

References

1. Eginhard & the Monk of St. Gall, *Early Lives of Charlemagne* (London: Chatto & Windus, 1926), 37–38.

2. Hamilton Wright Mabie and Kate Stephens, eds., *Heroes and Heroines Every Child Should Know* (New York: Doubleday, Page & Company, 1908), 275–276.

3. Clara Laughlin, *Foch the Man: A Life of the Supreme Commander of the Allied Armies* (New York, Fleming H. Revell Company, 1918), 101–102.

4. Plutarch, *Plutarch: The Lives of the Noble Grecians and Romans* (New York: The Modern Library, 1864), 185.

5. George Washington, *George Washington's Rules of Civility* (London, Chatto & Windus, 1890), 76.

6. Confucius.

7. William Shakespeare, *Hamlet, Act 1, Scene 3*, lines 70–72.

8. Washington, 112.

9. Ibid., 115.

Chapter 4

Articulate

adjective ar·tic·u·late \är-ˈti-kyə-lət\

1.

a : expressing oneself readily, clearly, and effectively • an articulate teacher; also: expressed in such a manner an articulate argument

b : divided into syllables or words meaningfully arranged : intelligible • an articulate cry/utterance

c : able to speak • So furious was he that he was hardly articulate. —Arthur Conan Doyle

2

a : consisting of segments united by joints: jointed articulate animals

b : distinctly marked off an articulate period in history

LV. In eloquence and in the art of war he either equalled or surpassed the fame of their most eminent representatives. . . .when Cicero reviews the orators in his Brutus, he says that he does not see to whom Caesar ought to yield the palm, declaring that his style is elegant as well as brilliant, even grand and in a sense noble. . . .He is said to have delivered himself in a high-pitched voice with impassioned action and gestures, which were not without grace. . . .

LVI. He left memoirs too of his deed in the Gallic war and in the civil strife with Pompey;. . .With regard to Caesar's memoirs Cicero, also in the Brutus speaks in the following terms: "He wrote memoirs which deserve the highest praise; they are naked in their simplicity, straightforward yet graceful, stripped of all rhetorical adornment, as of a garment."[1]

—*Suetonius, Roman historian, writing of Julius Caesar*

The Most Critical Trait?

There are three ways a leader can inspire others: presence, words, and action. Like all the traits mentioned in this book, none acts alone.

Aesop's fables are a collection of stories and each one teaches a lesson (a moral). They are believed to have been assembled during the Greek Empire between 600 BC and 500 BC. One fable applies specifically to having presence but not being articulate. In it, Aesop offers us a strong warning about how to ruin our presence by opening our mouth:

> An Ass once found a Lion's skin which the hunters had left out in the sun to dry. He put it on and went towards his native village. All fled at his approach, both men and animals, and he was a proud Ass that day. In his delight he lifted up his voice and brayed, but then every one knew him, and his owner came up and gave him a sound cudgelling for the fright he had caused. And shortly afterwards a Fox came up to him and said: "Ah, I knew you by our voice."
>
> Fine clothes may disguise, but silly words will disclose a fool.[2]

Written in more contemporary language, the moral might read: No matter how complete and distinguished your presence, you can open your mouth and convince everyone that you are an ass. The ability to communicate readily, clearly, and effectively in both speech and writing has been and will always be a distinguishing characteristic of leaders. A leader must be articulate. Wu Tzu wrote, "The leader of the army is one who is master of both arms and letters."[3] This was echoed by Suetonius, writing of Caesar and praising him "in eloquence and in the art of war,"[4] elaborating on this by later praising both his speaking and writing capabilities. Mastering words is as important as mastering your primary vocation. Survey respondents reinforced this by saying a leader is:

- a people person, listen and communicates well
- a person who is able to influence other people's actions, most effectively by convincing them of doing something they would not have done otherwise
- one who can inspire and direct others to give of themselves to reach a common goal
- one who communicates their vision clearly and then ensures their people have the resources to accomplish that vision

Take a look at the requirements for any job that includes supervisory responsibilities. Chances are it includes a phrase such as this:

- Must be able to communicate effectively in writing, over the phone, and with large groups
- Excellent communication skills (both oral and written)
- Good communication skills

Let's take a look at some of the key components that could help you understand and improve your ability to inspire through words.

The Basics of Communication

The purpose of communication is to transfer an image, thought, or vision to a receiving audience. Communication is a dialogue that exchanges information. If we believe that a leader should be visionary, that implies there is a vision that must be communicated to others so a group of people is pointed in the same direction. Ideally, you'll seek and obtain confirmation that others have understood your message. Without this, you may feel great about what you have said, but you won't know if others see it the same way you do.

Before discussing any elements of effective communication, it is imperative to acknowledge that articulate communication is primarily based in language. Ensure that you know the basics of the language in which you are trying to communicate. I hate to sound like your junior high school English teacher, but you *do* lose points for errors of diction, grammar, and punctuation—so don't make any.

Let's look at the other critical ingredients of communication, one at a time.

First, what is in a message?

There are five critical ingredients in any message, also known as the five Ws:

- Who – the sender and the receiver
- What – the important point(s) of a message
- When – the appropriate time
- Where – the place is the picture frame for the message
- Why – So what? Why should I listen to or read this?

In any speech or message that you come across, you should be able to find these elements. In every message you deliver, in person or in writing, you should ensure that you include these five elements. In fact, you should write them first. By doing so, "nice to have" traits such as "direct" and "straightforward" can be credited to your communication as you strive to be articulate.

In addition to the five Ws, state in very brief terms the desired outcome you are hoping to inspire through your communication, also known as the "vision" or "what you want it to look like when you're done." That is closely related to the *Why* of your message—your reason for communicating. If you can generate a vision and then accurately and simply describe the objective for your group, your team members may be able accomplish the objective without any further information. For this reason, being articulate is often the most visible "need to know" trait of leadership that you exercise.

Consider the following excerpt from the trial of Susan B. Anthony, an American suffragette who fought so women would have the right to vote.

This extract is from her defense while on trial for the charge of illegal voting at the presidential election of November 1872:

> **Miss Anthony**—May it please your honor, I am not arguing the question, but simply stating the reasons why sentence cannot, in justice, be pronounced against me. Your denial of my citizen's right to vote is the denial of my right of consent as one of the governed, the denial of my right of representation as one of the taxed, the denial of my right to a trial by a jury of my peers, as an offender against law, therefore, the denial of my sacred rights to life, liberty, property and—
>
> . . .
>
> **Judge Hunt**—The sentence of the Court is that you pay a fine of one hundred dollars and the costs of the prosecution.
>
> **Miss Anthony**—May it please your honor, I shall never pay a dollar of your unjust penalty. All the stock in trade I possess is a $10,000 debt, incurred by publishing my paper—*The Revolution*—four years ago, the sole object of which was to educate all women to do precisely as I have done, rebel against your manmade, unjust, unconstitutional forms of law, that tax, fine, imprison and hang women, while they deny them the right of representation in the government; and I shall work on with might and main to pay every dollar of that honest debt, but not a penny shall go to this unjust claim. And I shall earnestly and persistently continue to urge all women to the practical recognition of the old revolutionary maxim, that "Resistance to tyranny is obedience to God."[5]

During Anthony's argument in court, she explained why she was fighting and restated her vision: "to educate all women to do precisely as I have done, rebel."[6] Her vision was clear: that all women would have equal rights with men and that all women would participate in the fight until they had those equal rights. She died before the goal was reached, but her vision passed on. Women obtained the right to vote 14 years later.

Having confidence and credibility and including others are also key ingredients in a message that will resonate with those who hear it. These three elements are present in Anthony's statement to the court. Can you find them?

You could also refer to this example from President Ronald Reagan. In his farewell address, he used confidence, credibility, and inclusiveness in an exemplary manner:

And in all of that time I won a nickname, "The Great Communicator." But I never thought it was my style or the words I used that made a difference: it was the content. I wasn't a great communicator, but I communicated great things, and they didn't spring full bloom from my brow, they came from the heart of a great nation—from our experience, our wisdom, and our belief in the principles that have guided us for two centuries. They called it the Reagan revolution. Well, I'll accept that, but for me it always seemed more like the great rediscovery, a rediscovery of our values and our common sense.[7]

The entire speech reflects his confidence in himself and his performance as president. He includes everyone in the success with the repeated use of the word *our*. He reinforces his credibility by using a complimentary nickname that others had called him: the Great Communicator. Having confidence, credibility, and including others are key ingredients in a message that will resonate with those who receive it.

Be able to write out the five Ws for any message you craft, and then ensure that you demonstrate confidence, credibility, and inclusion of others as you communicate.

Second, a medium

There are two primary media for using words to inspire others: written and spoken.

The written word

Written words are signs made with the pen to represent and recall to the mind the spoken words (or voice-signs). Written language (that is, composition) must, of necessity, be somewhat fuller than spoken language, as well as more formal and exact. For the reader's understanding is not assisted by the tones of the voice, the changing expressions of the face, and the lively gestures, which help to make spoken language intelligible.[8]

—*An Advanced English Grammar*

Mastering the written word is no easy task, but as Suetonius wrote about Ceasar, there are some "nice to have" traits that can get you on the right track—plain, precise, elegant. You may have read a memo or letter in which a person overreaches their knowledge of the language they are using or uses too many words to say something. It's awkward. I have actually heard the word *disirregardlessly*. It's not a word. Read a grammar book to solidify and advance your knowledge of the language. In the meantime, follow these basic guidelines to improve the construction of your message.

You should be able to write one phrase or sentence for the *Who, What, Where, When,* and *Why* of your message (the five Ws). If you're covering more than one *What,* you should be able to generate a brief, bulleted list stating the *What* that you need to address. Keep it simple, whenever possible.

Use a format for your memo that is recognized by the people to whom you are writing. Many organizations use formatted messages, papers, and so on. If your organization does not have a format, find a format used by someone you respect and use it as a map or guide until you develop your own. When I was a staff officer in the Marine Corps, our unit had a manual that specified how every document should appear. One format was the Decision Paper. It contained: Executive Summary + Issue Statement + Discussion/Background + Recommendation. The requirement was to be able to put the whole argument on only one page, with the most valuable information summarized at the top. This format became useful during my MBA, as it put the answer up front for the professor to read but also had all the discussion available should the professor need to check my work. Many formats transcend organizations. Find one that works for you and be consistent in its application. Practice makes perfect.

Write the first and last parts after you've written everything else in your message. If the first part is not well written, some people will stop reading before they reach your argument. The last part is the opportunity for you to summarize and reiterate your key elements, which you can only accomplish after you have written everything else. It is also the last thing people read and may be the part they remember most clearly. If you read or watch speeches, you will see that the beginning and the conclusion are meant to draw attention and directly engage the audience in the message.

Obtain a critical review from someone who will point out your errors. One friend finding your errors in grammar, logic, or punctuation may sting a little, but it's better than the pain of launching your mistakes for public viewing. As Benjamin Franklin is alleged to have advised firefighters in Philadelphia, "an ounce of prevention is worth a pound of cure." That is equally applicable to writing.

This is also a good place to point out that the "written word" is changing. Anyone who has worked with data understands the benefit of generating an image that communicates a clear point. Dashboards, graphs, and so forth are all extensions of the written word and are excellent tools that can help you create an image of what is really important about what you are doing. Remember, keep it simple if you want it to be effective.

The spoken word

People want to be inspired. Being a good public speaker is key to inspiring those around you.

When it comes to public speaking, you construct the message just as you do when writing. While many dread public speaking, it is actually the easier way to communicate, as the previous quotation from the grammar textbook illustrates. You have numerous tools at your disposal for constructing and transmitting an image when speaking. Writing can only use words, but in public speaking you can use much more than words to share your vision with others. After you draft the five Ws of your message, consider the following tools for designing your presentation.

Props: If you want to leave an image in the mind of the listener, what might help you do that? During my run for vice president of the high school student council, each candidate was given a chance to address the student body of about 600 students. I got on stage wearing a hat made of poster board, which was just a very large square (2 ft x 2 ft) facing the audience. I introduced myself, told them that this box would be on their ballot, told them that my name would be on the ballot next to the box, and asked them to vote for me. I then slapped an enormous red check mark onto the box on my head and said, "Go to the polls and *check* it out!" The crowd loved it. Props speak for themselves and leave an image in the mind of the viewer that is hard to forget. In this case, that image was the vision I had—a check mark by my name on the ballot. Mine was the shortest speech, but it got me into the run-off election.

Wardrobe: How should you dress in order to be perceived as credible? As confident? As inclusive of others? People will even scrutinize the colors of your clothes based on your position and your message. Review the chapter on presence regarding clothing.

Scenery: Anything you have that can bring images related to your message into the mind of the listener can help you communicate. Having the right items to represent yourself, your message, or your cause is important. Showing someone a picture is great, but having something they can touch, use, or take is even more memorable since it involves more senses. It doesn't have to be complicated—a business card might be sufficient, depending on what is on it.

As you build your message to the audience, consider your non-verbals. Remember what was written about Caesar: "elegant as well as brilliant, even grand and in a sense noble." These movements are both scenery and punctuation marks to anything you are saying. People are constantly watching for your signals. Have you ever heard the question, "How much of our communication is in words?" I believe the scientific estimates hover near 25%. The remainder is in non-verbal cues that we send. If this is true (or even close to the truth), you have to plan and practice those movements that provide the emphasis you need to help convey your message or at least to keep people's attention. The way you move your body is an elemental part of being articulate and is also part of your presence.

Ensure that the words, tone, pitch, volume, and so forth are sufficient to carry your message. There is one common mistake here: many confuse "loudership" with "leadership." While you must speak loudly enough to be heard, being louder than others does not make you a leader. Talking too loudly is as bad as talking too much. Know when to be quiet or say nothing. Like any trait, beware of *too little* or *too much*.

Practice makes perfect, and again, asking a trusted friend or advisor for feedback can save you a lot of grief before you get up to speak.

Third, the dialogue

When I coached soccer, my audience was typically below the age of 10. I also coached high school players. There is little comparison between the message I crafted for the children and for the young adults. The *what* of the message was the same—the rules and technical skills of soccer are constants. The vocabularies, skill levels (or knowledge levels), and attention spans of the audiences were completely different. The audience is your indicator as to *how* you build your message and choose your words, as well as how you receive feedback.

Feedback is a key part of communication. If you are attempting to provide information, communicate a message, or share a vision, you should seek information that confirms that the message was received. In the case of coaching, the feedback came from watching the players. Their level of understanding was evident in their actions. I often had to recraft the message and try again with some of my players. Some players could easily absorb verbal instructions, while others benefited from a demonstration of the skill. Many times, repeating the visual demonstration in a sort of slow motion was the key to successful communication.

Teachers constantly craft messages, send them, and seek confirmation of understanding. As you can imagine, *how* they do this is dependent on the age of their audience. A teacher's ability to craft and communicate information is typically well developed because they have practiced with numerous audiences. Their capability in this leadership trait helps us understand one reason why several participants in the survey named teachers or professors when asked to "name one person that you think of when you hear the word *leader*."

When you speak or write, develop a way to determine if your vision was understood. When speaking to an audience, be attentive to what the expressions of the listeners are telling you. If the expression matches what you are communicating, that is good. If you say something intended as humor and they aren't laughing, that is not good. Are you serious? Look for gravity in the viewers. Are you smiling? Look for smiles in return. If you ask a question, does anyone try to answer? There are many indicators of whether an audience is "with you."

Obtaining feedback from writing is more difficult, but not impossible. If you send an email or a letter (that was what we sent before electronic mail, or email), you can ask questions next time you talk to the recipient, whether on the phone or in person. You can choose to end the correspondence with a question. That works especially well in message apps and emails, where people can answer back quickly. You can also observe to see if action was taken that shows receipt and agreement with your last message.

Conclusion

Leadership doesn't exist without the participation of others. Communication is the multi-function tool that leaders use to learn the needs of the team, to communicate the vision that the team develops, and to obtain the feedback to know that everyone is on course. Expressing yourself readily, clearly, and effectively—being articulate—takes a studious effort by anyone who seeks a leadership role or finds themselves recruited into one. Being articulate aids in daily communication, negotiation, feedback, and public speaking (think: inspiring others). When you are absent, your written correspondence represents you. While this chapter has focused primarily on the quality of your communication, always remember that the quantity is equally important. Know when to stop talking. More is not always better. As Aesop told us, "Silly words will disclose a fool."[9]

It takes willingness on your part to solicit and obtain feedback, and it takes humility to accept the messages that come in that feedback—for better or worse. That ties communication to other key traits—compassion and service.

Don't be *unintelligible*. Be *articulate*, but not so articulate that *you become pretentious*. And don't *lose the message by using too many words*.

Food for Thought

Read this:

1. The original transcripts of the speeches and letters of Dr. Martin Luther King, Jr. are available online. Do you feel that King projects confidence, credibility, and inclusion in his writing? If yes, how does he do it?

2. An inaugural address is the first opportunity for a newly elected president to begin a dialogue with various audiences. Choose a president you don't know much about and read his inaugural address. Can you identify the elements and audiences of his message?

3. Download a book on grammar. There are several online that are free. *How to Speak and Write Correctly* and *An Advanced English Grammar with Exercises* are quoted in this chapter. Alternatively, access a website that teaches grammar. Read every chapter and do every exercise. If you are going to communicate, *don't lose points for errors of diction, grammar, or punctuation.*

4. Read *The Art of Public Speaking* by Dale Carnegie, also available for free online.

Watch this:

1. Watch a speech online. During a speech, you do not usually have the opportunity to pick the scenery, the setting, or the props. What, in your opinion, makes the speech effective, despite being unable to change the setting? Listen carefully for parts of the speech that conjure up images that generate visual scenery in the minds of the listeners.

Do this:

1. Let someone proofread a difficult email. That requires humility, but you can't correct errors that you don't see. Get the best writer you know to proofread your composition whenever you can. See what you learn.

2. Practice a presentation in front of a willing audience (even if "willing" means "because you bought them a soda"). The investment will be worth it.

References

1. Gaius Suetonius Tranquillus, *Suetonius I*, Trans. J. C. Rolfe, eds. T. E. Tage and W. H. D. Rouse (London: William Heinemann and the Macmillan Co., 1908), 75–77.

2. Joseph Jacobs, *The Fables of Aesop* (London: MacMillan & Co., 1912), 116.

3. Sunzi and Wutzu, 76.

4. Suetonius, 75.

5. An Account of the Proceedings on the Trial of Susan B. Anthony, on the Charge of Illegal Voting, at the Presidential Election in November, 1872 and on the Trial of Beverly W. Jones, Edwin T. Marsh and William B. Hall, The Inspectors of Election by Whom Her Vote was Received (Rochester, NY: Daily Democrat and Chronicle Book Print, 1874), 82, 85.

6. Ibid.

7. Ronald Reagan, "Farewell Address to the Nation," January 11, 1989. *The American Presidency Project*, accessed January 12, 2018 at http://www.presidency.ucsb.edu/ws/index.php?pid=29650.

8. George Lyman Kittredge and Frank Edgar Farley, *An Advanced English Grammar*, (Boston: Ginn and Company, 1913), xii.

9. Jacobs, 116.

Chapter 5

Compassion

noun com·pas·sion \kəm-ˈpa-shən\
: **sympathetic consciousness of others' distress together with a desire to alleviate it**

The most essential thing in the world to any individual is to understand himself. The next is to understand the other fellow. For life is largely a problem of running your own car as it was built to be run, plus getting along with the other drivers on the highway.[1]

—Elsie Lincoln Benedict and Ralph Paine Benedict,
How to Analyze People on Sight

In their book *How to Analyze People on Sight*, the Benedicts put forth an interesting theory on how to understand the people around you. In the introduction, they offer this image of cars and getting along with others.

Sharing the Highway of Life

Any way you look at it, you can't be a leader without other people. Rarely do people stay in leadership very long if they can't understand the motivations, abilities, and hopes of the people around them. Compassion in leadership is the ability to perceive or discern things about others and want to do something about them. There are many ways that this quality is captured in modern society and many labels attached to it—emotional intelligence, empathy, soft skills, sensitivity, social intelligence. *Compassion* is the word that sums up all of these and, like the other traits in this book, has elements that are understandable if considered carefully.

The survey participants called out compassion and some of its components in their definitions of leadership. A leader is:

- a good listener
- adaptable to the needs of the people they are in charge of
- compassionate
- someone who puts other's needs before themselves
- someone that cares for his/her team
- someone that cares for those they are leading
- someone who can understand others and help in need
- someone who can handle being pressured, understand both situations before jumping to conclusions, empathetic to their people and does not put a blanket over the truth, no matter how terrible it is

- someone who knows when to lead and when to take a step back and let his/her team to do the Job. He/She must have high EQ.

Compassion has been and will always be a key to understanding and relating to the people around us. Every person you meet is unique. Compassion helps you recognize the abilities of others, encourage them to contribute in a way that maximizes their potential, and move them toward achieving their individual and team goals.

If you're not working with the people around you, if you're in it for yourself or you feel better going it alone, you're not being a leader.

γνῶθι σεαυτόν—Know Thyself

The idea to *know thyself* was originally studied by Greek philosophers. Consider the following lines of Greek philosopher Socrates, recorded by Xenophon in his *Memorobilia*, written in the fourth century BC:

> Is it not clear too that through self-knowledge men come to much good, and through self-deception to much harm? For those who know themselves, know what things are expedient for themselves and discern their own powers and limitations. And by doing what they understand, they get what they want and prosper: by refraining from attempting what they do not understand, they make no mistakes and avoid failure. And consequently through their power of testing other men too, and through their intercourse with others, they get what is good and shun what is bad. Those who do not know and are deceived in their estimate of their own powers, are in the like condition with regard to other men and other human affairs. They know neither what they want, nor what they do, nor those with whom they have intercourse; but mistaken in all these respects, they miss the good and stumble into the bad.[2]

Socrates said a lot about the value of knowing yourself. Know your needs. Know your strengths. Know your limits. He also points out the importance of recognizing what you do not know.

It may seem vain to see your world in a way that puts you at the center, but it is the place where we all begin relating to others. Since childhood, we have each worked to understand the world around us—what can hurt us, what can help us, what we like, what we don't like. It is only through ourselves that we relate to our surroundings, and those surroundings include people. You are the constant reference point as you move from team to team, from place to place, or from project to project. Everything you see is in relation to you. What you see from your reference point is your point of view. Since self-knowledge is the starting point in every relationship you will have, both personally and professionally, knowing yourself is the only place to begin to understand others. When you meet someone new, you are evaluating them. Is this person a threat? Is this person someone I want on my team? The first question is allegedly part of our development and survival. We are sensitive to threats against our well-being, and sometimes that threat comes in the form of a person. The second question deals with utility and our agendas. Both of these relate to your well-being and your advantage. Leadership is taking your point of view away from your advantage and shifting it to the advantage of the team. It is exchanging an "I" for a "we."

Make sure you learn as much about yourself as possible and be honest about what you find. I recognize those parts of my thoughts that were formed by my 24 years as a Marine, by how my family brought me up, and by my academic studies. In short, my experience has affected the way I think about things, and I must recognize this. I remind myself that I can only learn more if I accept the questions and observations of those around me. I am not the smartest person in the room. Anyone around me can teach me something new, and sometimes that has to do with my character. Part of knowing yourself is allowing people to shine a flashlight into the dark recesses of your character to make you explore those places. Rather than see this as criticism, see it as an opportunity to challenge your own beliefs and get to know yourself a little better. You are the reference point by which you measure others, so make sure you can read the measurements clearly.

While knowing yourself is the place to begin, it is not the place to finish. If you only take this first step, you may become self-centered, which is a poor start to leadership. Move on to the next step—knowing others.

Listen and Observe

If you want to learn how people think, ask them. Listen and watch them as they articulate their thoughts on any subject. The words they say are important. How they say them is even more important. Listen, learn, and know how the people around you think and respond.

Listening is similar to being articulate. To be articulate while speaking, you must properly use your language, your body language, and changes in your voice to communicate a vision to others. To listen well, closely observe the language, the body language, and the voice of others so you understand the vision they have in their mind. What makes listening more difficult is determining if what you are hearing is the truth, the speaker's understanding of the truth, or something they know isn't true.

Don't be discouraged if you listen and misunderstand. That is part of the process of getting to know someone. It takes time and practice, like any other skill.

There are numerous articles online that contain tips to become a better listener, but I'll put one tip here that you may not find in articles and blogs. Try. If you ask a question, wait and listen for the answer rather than thinking of your next response or riposte. Remember, you are not only listening for the information the answer may contain, but you are watching for the thought process behind the words.

Relate

If you know about yourself and you know about others, you can relate. I recommend that you make every effort to find areas of overlap. That is, find and focus on areas that you have in common with someone else. I guarantee that no matter how much you may not like someone after getting a first impression, if you earnestly seek to find things you have in common, you will find them, and the opportunity to form a relationship will be there.

When I first became a flight instructor, I worked hard to learn the syllabus, the maneuvers, the grading system, the aircraft—all the technical things I needed to know. I started flying with students and felt like I was doing well. After all, I had a degree in aerospace engineering, and I was a pilot, so I was a great instructor, right? After a few months of teaching, a senior instructor pulled me aside and offered me some advice. "If you want to be a good teacher, remember what it was like to be a student." In a flash, I remembered how much I initially suffered from airsickness, confusion, and uncertainty when I started flight training. I remembered that being a pilot had been my dream for as long as I could recall, and I remembered worrying about whether I was going to make it through the program. His advice forced me to relate to the students as individuals with hopes, problems, and concerns about whether they were going to make it through the program. Once I learned that, I changed my whole approach to teaching. I took the time to find out each student's motivation, where they were in the process, and where they were having issues. More importantly, I realized that it was my job and my privilege to help them get where they wanted to go. I flew with students who suffered from airsickness, just like I had. I flew with students who were a little uncomfortable with aerobatics, just like I had been. I flew with students who weren't sure they were going to make it, just like I wasn't. When I began to relate to my students, I became part of *their* team. I did my best to help every one of them, even if I flew with them just once during their time in training.

No matter what your role is right now, you can listen and find areas in which you and those around you are similar, as well as areas in which you are not. When you find areas of difference, don't assume that your point of view is right or better. There may be an opportunity to let others teach you something about yourself. Give them a chance to help you understand their way of thinking. There may also be an opportunity to practice compassion if you hear them express an area in which you can help. If you help someone reach their goals, you're helping the team reach its goal, and you will have something in common—shared success.

Relating is where teambuilding begins. Understanding yourself and the other members of your team lets you identify areas where the team will be comfortable working together and areas where there may be some disagreement. Understanding how members of your group can find common ground lets you identify and strengthen bonds between your team members. When you're leading the group, you can begin to achieve and celebrate small successes in the areas of agreement while working to understand the underlying reasons for the differences. If you listen well, you can find ways to obtain agreement. Even if you don't have enough time to find complete agreement, trying to understand the others around you will lead to a way forward, together. In the end, compassion is about listening and helping. Finding a way to help the team along, despite its differences, is an ongoing exercise in compassion.

Conclusion

Be compassionate about what others understand. People will follow you (or not) based on their understanding of leadership, not yours. Do you want to be a good leader? Remember what it was like to be a follower or team member. Some survey participants wrote that leaders are:

- Powerful and dominant
- Bullish, controlling, and self-centered an enlightened despot
- The person who speaks up first. Alternatively, the person who speaks loudest. The manipulator, required to galvanize lazy/cowardly sods to action

---

We all know that this type of leader exists and that we'll meet people like them in the future. Two of the above respondents answered yes when asked, "Do you want to be like this person?" indicating that there will likely be more leaders like this.

Compassion isn't about trying not to offend, avoiding difficult topics, or being politically correct. It is about keeping your focus outward rather than on yourself. When you are leading an effort, you will share in the difficulties your people are facing. You will face challenges together with your team, and you will have complications with some of the people around you. Having conversations based on a fear that you may hurt someone's feelings won't get to the heart of the matter. Ask honest questions, listen to the answers, find the areas you have in common and the areas of difference, and find a way to bridge the gaps. Remember, the goal of compassion is to alleviate difficulties or, as the definition states, alleviate distress. Everyone on your team will have a bad day at some point, including you. Modeling compassion is how you enable the team to help each other and to help you when times are tough. A team that helps each other is much stronger than a team that does not. You can lead the strongest team by working to understand everyone around you and modeling compassion.

Listen to where there is distress and work to alleviate it. If you want to embrace leadership as your future, understand compassion and prepare for a life of service, but remember the warning of Sun Tzu "over-regard for the troops . . . causes inconvenience."[3]

Don't *be blind to the needs of others*. Be *compassionate*, but not so compassionate that *you are over concerned about comfort*. And don't *make compassion your only focus—you have work to do*.

Food for Thought

Read this:

1. Read the mission statements of five non-profit organizations. Examples include the Bill and Melinda Gates Foundation, the International Committee of the Red Cross, and Compassion International. There are many others. How many organizations can you find that are leaders in their field and also make compassion and service their purpose?

Watch this:

1. Use a video search engine to find Pope Francis I speaking on humble leadership. Does he mention compassion? If so, in what capacity?

Do this:

1. There are several online tests available that enable you to learn about yourself. Personality types and the insight they provide can be the first step in understanding yourself. As we've already discussed, once you understand yourself, you can begin to understand and relate to others. Take one of the free personality tests and read the results—all of them. What do you agree with? What do you disagree with? Why?

2. The next time someone says something about your character that you don't like, don't say anything. Imagine that what they are saying is true and see if you can determine why. Ask them why they said it. Take the opportunity to know thyself. If you learn something, thank the person who brought it to your attention.

References

1. Elsie Lincoln Benedict and Ralph Paine Benedict, *How to Analyze People on Sight* (East Aurora, NY: Roycrofters, 1921), 11.

2. *Xenophon Memorabilia Oeconomicus Symposium Apology*, trans. E.C. Marchant (Cambridge, MA: Harvard University Press, 1923), 287–289.

3. Sunzi and Wutzu, 46.

Chapter 6

Service-minded

noun ser·vice \ˈsər-vəs\

1

a : the occupation or function of serving • in active service

b : employment • as a servant entered his service

2

a : the work performed by one that serves • good service

b : help, use, benefit • glad to be of service

c : contribution to the welfare of others

d : disposal for use • I'm entirely at your service

3

a : a form followed in worship or in a religious ceremony • the burial service

b : a meeting for worship—often used in plural • held evening services

4

: the act of serving: such as

a : a helpful act • did him a service

b : useful labor that does not produce a tangible commodity—usually used in plural • charge for professional services

c : serve

First Is Last

Why can one team, unit, or organization overpower and outperform similar teams, units, or organizations when similarly equipped and similarly sized? It comes down to the abilities and efforts of the people in the group. This is one of the greatest challenges for some new leaders to accept—*it is not all about you*. The definition at the beginning of this chapter—*contribution to the welfare of others*—is how service enhances a group of people. By contributing to the well-being and growth of each member of the team, you contribute to the growth and accomplishments of the whole team.

As a leader, you will be responsible for other people. Your success will be measured by the success of the people you lead. If you help them be their best and do their best, the office or team will perform at its best. Your service is to enable and inspire the people around you to be the best version of themselves they can be. Leadership is like parenting. You are taking care of those around you and helping them grow.

Consider some of the many service-minded definitions from the survey participants. A Leader is:

- a servant first and a grower for future leaders
- a servant of his team and their objectives
- a servant of others! Someone who understands the needs of others and offers help and guidance!
- a servant, supporting and empowering those who work for her/him
- a server
- a person who helps others grow
- someone who guides you to a better place or teaches you something that will help you grow
- someone who is more interested to remove barriers and help people to achieve their best than to build an altar to himself
- here to help his team grow
- a person who helps others grow
- someone who brings the best of his/her team members by supporting them, bringing them up, nourishing their strengths
- someone who is selfless

- someone whose goal is to grow and build others so they are better versions of themselves. A leader is humble, empathetic, and always learning and growing.
- the one who gives the people the tools to succeed

The sheer number of definitions that described service highlights the modern appetite for servant leaders. There is an ardent desire to work for leaders who will help people grow. Being a servant doesn't put you beneath anyone, and it doesn't mean you are weak. You *choose* to serve. You act on this choice for the benefit of those around you and, ultimately, for your team's effort and success.

Contributing to the Welfare of Others

Being attuned to those around you is not a 21st-century accomplishment. Remember Florence Nightingale? Even though I chose to use part of her story in the chapter on presence, it could have just as easily been included here. As a nurse, she was well attuned to the distress of others. Her service was to alleviate suffering as much as possible. She exemplified presence, compassion, and service, equipping both doctors and nurses to do their part in relieving distress.

Mothers, nurses, fathers, and nuns made the list of leaders in the survey. In so many ways, their first task is to serve. If being service-minded still seems like an odd fit for leadership, consider this example. If you're driving a car and you are low on gas, are you going to get more? If you run out, how will you continue on your journey? As a leader, one of the engines that moves you forward is the efforts of those around you. If they are "running out of gas" (motivation, energy, clarity, etc.), are you willing to bring them more, or do you expect them to get it themselves? If one of them runs out completely, what will you do to help them rejoin the team? Taking action to keep your team and its assets moving forward is often how you help the team. By choosing to serve, you enable others to keep moving.

A coach cannot step on the field and win a game. Only the players can do that. Several coaches were listed in the survey, even though they are restricted to teaching and enabling the players. The coach must make sure the players have what they need to step onto the field and win. They do that not just by imparting knowledge but by ensuring proper nutrition, treating injuries, and building team spirit—all acts of service that must happen on a successful sports team.

Consider the following story about Admiral Lord Nelson, who spent his career in Her Majesty's Royal Navy, distinguishing himself on multiple occasions for courage, tactics, and leadership, especially during the Napoleonic Wars.

> Nelson's first business after he got to London, even before he went to see his relations, was to attempt to get the wages due to his men, for the various ships in which they had served during the war. "The disgust of seamen to the navy," he said, "was all owing to the infernal plan of turning them over from ship to ship; so that men could not be attached to the officers, nor the officers care the least about the men." Yet he himself was so beloved by his men, that his whole ship's company offered, if he could get a ship, to enter for her immediately.[1]

He chose to act on behalf of those he had led. He chose to serve the sailors who would, in turn, serve him. He exercised his moral courage to ensure that the men were paid the wages they were owed, despite the absence of records and the perceived absence of concern from other officers in the Royal Navy.

Task = Tools + Time + Training

A pneumonic I have used through the latter part of my career is that if you give anyone a task, you must ensure that they have the tools, the time, and the training they need to accomplish the task. Consider the alternative. You give someone a task for which they are unprepared and ill-equipped. What is the probability of success? Part of your job as a leader is to track successes and failures and determine how much of each failure is your responsibility. Did the people on the task have the right resources? Were they given a reasonable amount of time to analyze the task, develop a way ahead, and move forward? Was there any required knowledge related to this task that was not provided?

Most leaders manage a budget and can allocate one of the principle ingredients of modern business solutions: money. It can be invested into training, tools, and other resources. If you consider the tasks that you most often need to accomplish, that gives you insight into areas where that money could be best spent. Are the tools and training of your people sufficient? If not, what are *you* going to do about it?

It's Not All About You

Among her many accomplishments, Clara Barton established the American Branch of the International Red Cross. While we can see the impact of the American Red Cross today, look at the obscurity it held when it was first realized:

> All this had been accomplished by the kindly help of a few personal friends, tireless and unrewarded, and while the news of the accession of the Government of the United States, to the treaty of Geneva, lit bonfires that night (for I cabled it by their request) in the streets of Switzerland, France, Germany, and Spain, a little four-line paragraph in the congressional doings of the day in the *Evening Star*, of Washington, alone announced to the people of America that an international treaty had been added to their rolls.
>
> No personal distinction had been bestowed, no one honored, no one politically advanced, no money of the Government expended, and, like other things of like nature and history, it was left in obscurity to make its own way and live its own hard life.
>
> Thus the spring of 1882 found us—a few people, tired and weak, with five years of costly service.[2]

Look closely at the list of acknowledgments received by the people who made the American Red Cross possible:

- no personal distinction had been bestowed
- no one honored
- no one politically advanced
- no money of the government expended

At its beginning, the American Red Cross was utterly invisible and its leaders were even more so. Of the leadership challenges faced by Clara Barton and her volunteers, this was one of the greatest: to serve others without notice, appreciation, or reward. Not only had five years of effort been expended to obtain the necessary treaty, but the early regulations in her organization promised no future reward either.

Consider the guidelines she set out:

First. To never solicit relief or ask for contributions.

Second. Not to pay salaries to officers—paying out money only to those whom we must employ for manual labor—and as our officers served without compensation they should not be taxed for dues.

Third. To keep ourselves always in possession of a stated sum of money to commence a field of disaster—this sum to be independent even of the closed doors of a bank which might prevent leaving for a field on a Sunday or holiday.[3]

Could the Red Cross have developed into the organization we now know if its founders had been unwilling to take on the leadership trait of being service-minded? How many organizations could run on these principles today? Can you?

Do you see the value of these simple guidelines and the clarity they provide to the people in the organization? Part of leadership and service is ensuring that people around you are never left without direction. When in doubt, any team member can work in a way that aligns with the values or regulations of an organization. Well-written (articulate) regulations such as those written by Clara Barton are a guiding force for people when leaders are temporarily absent. Part of your task is to ensure that instructions are available whenever someone may have doubt about the way ahead. Values and an articulated vision also provide this, especially when making decisions for or about a company. Like a compass, values point the way. In a dynamic environment, writing a clear vision of a desired end-state is a key service that leaders provide because it helps people work, without doubt, toward the team's objective.

Like anything, there can be too little or too much direction. Too little results in wasted effort since people are unsure of what to do next. Too much results in micro-managing the actions of others, which is typically not well received and may discourage independent, creative action by your team members. Having values or regulations written out is useful if the people within the organization know them and are able to act upon them. They should be short enough to read but long enough to transmit the message.

Conclusion

The danger that faces and defeats so many leaders is the mistaken belief that "it's all about me." There is no doubt that the right leader at the right time can make an enormous difference for a group of people, but the truth remains that the efforts of the group—every member—make success possible, achieve a victory, and win the game. When you *choose* to serve, you enable your teammates to be better. When everyone on the team is better—psychologically, physically, technically, tactically—performance soars. If you want to lead the best team, it is your duty to give every member access to the time, tools, and training necessary to improve themselves and complete the task at hand. You have work to do every day. Listen to the team's needs and equip them for the task at hand.

Marine officers have embraced a practice that reminds them daily that they should be servant-leaders. At mealtimes, officers are to be served last. If there is no food left, the officer knows he or she should plan better for the care of the Marines. My most memorable meal was on the island of Iwo Jima. I had arranged for meals to come ashore at lunchtime to feed my detachment of Marines and sailors that were there to execute an anniversary event. What was left for me at the end? A cup of rice, a slice of bread, and a packet of peanut butter. Note to self: Plan for more food to come ashore tomorrow so everyone stays fueled up and ready to go.

Don't be *self-centered.* Be *service-minded,* but not so service-minded that *you fail to perform your other duties.* And don't *ever think that it is all about you.*

Food for Thought

Read this:

1. Which leader named in the appendix best exhibits the trait of being service-minded? Why? Are there leaders on the list whose names you don't recognize? Choose three that you don't know and read about them. Do they exhibit this trait?
2. Clara Barton's selfless efforts were exemplary of what it is to be a servant-leader. Many other people have also led in this way, but I encourage you to read her book about the story of the founding of the American Red Cross—*A Story of*

the Red Cross: Glimpses of Field Work. You will see key traits of leadership expressed throughout.

Watch this:

1. Type "servant leadership" into a video search engine. The number of results may surprise you. Pick one speaker you know and like and one speaker you do not know. Watch as they present their views on the subject.

Do this:

1. Whether you are currently in a leadership position or not, choose an opportunity to serve, and do it. We all have work to do, but sometimes you can help another person in a way that has a small cost to you but provides an enormous benefit to them. Find one of these opportunities today, try to enable growth through service, and see how it goes. While I encourage serving your community, in this case I mean an action in your daily life—in your school, office, family, or team. Serve another person in a way that gives them an opportunity to excel. Here are some examples:

   - Take a task from another person's to-do list that is easy for you so they have more time to focus on something that is difficult for them.
   - Help someone with their current training (or class) so they can be well prepared to help the team.
   - Provide training in something you know well to someone who struggles with that skill or topic.
   - If you're on a team and training together for an event, work or study with someone who needs the extra motivation.

   The objective of this is *not* to sacrifice yourself for someone else's advantage, but to contribute to their success in a way that doesn't take you off track.

References

1. Robert Southey, *The Life of Horatio Lord Nelson* (London: J.M. Dent & Sons, 1906), 24–25.

2. Clara Barton, *A Story of the Red Cross: Glimpses of Field Work* (New York: D. Appleton and Company, 1907), 5.

3. Ibid., 10–11.

Chapter 7

Intelligent

noun in·tel·li·gence \in-ˈte-lə-jən(t)s\

1

a (1) : the ability to learn or understand or to deal with new or trying situations : reason; also : the skilled use of reason

(2) : the ability to apply knowledge to manipulate one's environment or to think abstractly as measured by objective criteria (such as tests)

b : Christian science : the basic eternal quality of divine mind

c : mental acuteness : shrewdness

2

a : an intelligent entity; especially : angel

b : intelligent minds or mind • cosmic intelligence

3

: the act of understanding : comprehension

4

a : information, news

b : information concerning an enemy or possible enemy or an area; also : an agency engaged in obtaining such information

5

: the ability to perform computer functions

The Foundation of Success

Intelligence deals with the speed at which you can attain new knowledge. There are many ways to obtain knowledge—education or experience, for example. Intelligence is what allows you to change the experience into knowledge and then retain and communicate it.

In Benjamin Franklin's autobiography, he mentioned several libraries. Among these was the collection of books his father had, a library he saw at the governor's house, a collection of books shared among a group of his father's friends, and the first public subscription library in the United States. Franklin gave significant importance to the impact of libraries on his development. He valued access to knowledge and the opportunity to use it. Today, the internet serves as a collection of information so large that it seems daunting. The information is ever-ready and ever-available. Supply has greatly exceeded demand, so information seems cheap. But imagine life before the internet (some readers won't have to imagine). The network of information was libraries where books could be traded or shared and where information was made available to the public. Having access to a good library was a path to success. Benjamin Franklin celebrated his access to libraries, and so did Alexander the Great, Andrew Carnegie, Booker T. Washington, and many others. Knowledge was and is a key to success.

Think of someone you consider a leader. Do you think they are more intelligent than you? More knowledgeable? You may believe a leader is more knowledgeable or intelligent simply because you expect that to be true. Rarely do we want to follow someone because we believe they are ignorant, so we believe them to be intelligent. Look at some of the definitions of leadership from the survey:

- charismatic and knowledgeable
- knowledgeable
- someone who has self-knowledge, intelligence and human sense
- an expert
- someone who knows the way and how to get there

- someone who has visionary view, has been focusing in one field for many years. He/she knows the industry very well. A leader must know his stuff very well and is good at motivating the potential talent of the employee and knows how to dispatch the most qualified candidate to the right position.

Even though we suffer from information-overload in the Information Age, access to and use of education and knowledge remains a key opportunity for any prospective leader to exercise intelligence and move ahead.

"Get Wisdom. Though It Cost All You Have, Get Understanding"

King Solomon was considered by some to be the wisest person who ever lived. He wrote about the importance of gaining understanding and knowledge in his Proverbs.

> Then [my father] taught me, and he said to me,
> "Take hold of my words with all your heart;
> keep my commands, and you will live.
> Get wisdom, get understanding;
> do not forget my words or turn away from them.
> Do not forsake wisdom, and she will protect you;
> love her, and she will watch over you.[1]

Winston Churchill made similar observations as a young war correspondent in 1897. While deployed with the British army, he included a chapter of general observations and explained their utility to the reader:

> It may at first seem, that a chapter wholly devoted to military considerations is inappropriate to a book which, if it is to enjoy any measure of success, must be read by many unconnected with the army. But I remember that in these days it is necessary for every one, who means to be well informed, to have a superficial knowledge of every one else's business.[2]

Notice that neither Solomon nor Churchill specified one type of learning or one branch of learning taking precedence over another. They simply refer to knowledge, wisdom, or knowing something about everybody's business. In the survey, at least one respondent specified that the leader should "know the industry very well," implying that specific knowledge is also valued.

In addition to "knowing the industry," someone who works with others must obtain knowledge about people—themselves first and then others. The concept of understanding people is covered in the chapter on compassion.

Two Types of Knowledge

Broad knowledge

If you read the autobiography of Benjamin Franklin, you will find that he taught himself four European languages and Latin. He also studied philosophy, ethics, politics, history, and many other subjects; hence the importance of libraries for him. Some would see that as a waste of time. If your industry is a modern one such as petroleum, mobile apps, or manufacturing, why study Latin or philosophy?

Multiple studies show the benefits of learning. Learning makes you more able to learn, helps you ward off certain illnesses of the mind, and helps some mental processes become more agile. In short, you can become more intelligent and increase the speed at which you take up information.

In a leadership situation, the ability to gather information rapidly contributes to another leadership ability: decisiveness. Making right decisions is central to leadership, and having correct information enables you to make better decisions. While everyone can learn from failure, people typically want to follow someone who "knows the way and how to get there," as someone wrote in the survey. Even the statement "know the way" is loaded with knowledge requirements. A simple, historical translation of knowing the way would require reading a map, identifying a route, following directions, and so on. Applied to any other settling, it reveals that accomplishing any one thing could require knowing many things, or being broadly knowledgeable. Not only does learning enable future learning, but knowing more is how you broaden the skill set that you have.

You don't always know which specific skill will best support your team effort, so be best prepared by learning broadly.

Specific knowledge

If I am going on an international flight, I am not really interested in knowing that the pilot speaks Italian, can bake a soufflé, or assembles dune buggies as a hobby. I really hope that the pilot can operate the aircraft. Often, specific knowledge is necessary for specific success. Consider the following case with a chemist hired by Andrew Carnegie, who built the American steel empire:

> We found the man in a learned German, Dr. Fricke, and great secrets did the doctor open up to us. Iron stone from mines that had a high reputation was now found to contain ten, fifteen, and even twenty per cent less iron than it had been credited with. Mines that hitherto had a poor reputation we found to be now yielding superior ore. The good was bad and the bad was good, and everything was topsy-turvy. Nine tenths of all the uncertainties of pig-iron making were dispelled under the burning sun of chemical knowledge. . . .
>
> What fools we had been! But then there was this consolation: we were not as great fools as our competitors. It was years after we had taken chemistry to guide us that it was said by the proprietors of some other furnaces that they could not afford to employ a chemist. Had they known the truth then, they would have known that they could not afford to be without one.[3]

The chemist made the steelmaking processes more efficient by determining the quality of the ingredients. The end result was a better product with errors removed by the "burning sun of chemical knowledge."

One of the survey respondents wrote that a leader "knows the industry very well." Becoming an expert in your field will attract others. If you are the most knowledgeable, you may also be the most capable when accomplishing tasks in your specialty. Knowing more can put you in a position to attract students. That is a leadership position. In the case of Carnegie, knowledge made him even more successful, eventually employing and leading more people.

While knowing a lot about one thing is necessary for the success of many projects, you cannot be blind to things that affect the area in which you are an expert. Returning to the example of a pilot, while I served in that capacity, I was initially expected to just fly the plane safely from point A to point B. Then I learned other capabilities of the aircraft and was expected to perform those when required. Finally, as an aircraft commander, I was ultimately responsible for the safe operation of the aircraft—all of it. That meant that I had to know how to operate the aircraft, but I also had to know how everyone on board affected what I was doing. I had to learn every step of each emergency procedure so I knew *who* was doing *what* and how it affected my ability to operate the aircraft. That's why the Pilot-in-Command has final say on the operations of the aircraft. The pilot works very hard to be very knowledgeable about the aircraft and is ultimately responsible.

Be specifically and deeply knowledgeable about your area of expertise, and know how things around you can affect what you are doing. Be the expert, but don't be isolated, thinking that what you know is all there is to know.

The Danger of Knowledge

If you get caught reading a book, you may be asked, "What are you reading?" The reaction to your answer will vary based on what you are reading, but just being known as a reader may lead others to believe that you seek knowledge and are, therefore, very smart. Don't let your quest for knowledge make you proud. Knowledge is a critical part of being intelligent and being a leader. But service is another key component of leadership, and pride prevents being service-minded.

Another danger of seeking knowledge is believing that you are ahead of others. The moment you believe you are the smartest person in the room, you may cease to listen to the ideas of others. As a leader, listening to those around you is critical to success. Imagine leading an organization of 25,000 people. Do you really know more about every job than the people who perform them? If you ever believe you are the most intelligent person in the room, you critically injure your ability to learn from the others around you and incorporate their knowledge to help when solving a problem.

In 2009, I was assigned as the Officer-in-Charge of a detachment that would support the ceremony commemorating the 65th anniversary of the Battle of Iwo Jima. I would be working in cooperation with the Japanese Maritime Self-Defense Force garrison on the island. It would take months of planning and involve moving one Navy ship; 250 Marines, sailors, and civilians; 43 vehicles; and a dozen aircraft in support of 56 US veterans of the battle, 17 Japanese veterans, 200 US tourists, 30 US distinguished guests, and 138 members of the US Marine Corps Battle Colors Detachment, all onto the Pacific Island of Iwo Jima (now called Iwo To). During the planning, there was one problem for which I had no solution: we had seven seven-ton trucks available that could move 22 people at a time, but the bed of the truck was six feet (two meters) off the ground. Marines would typically have no problem scrambling up into the truck, but we believed the guests and veterans would be unable to do that. The average age of the tourists was approximately 50, and the average veteran was over 85. How would we get the tourists into the trucks for movement around the island? I researched every option I could but was unable to develop a solution. So I put the problem to the planning team. The solution came from the 20-year-old corporal who led the engineering detachment. He said that if I could get someone to provide lumber, his team could build staircases that could be lifted into place at each of the stops on the route we designed for transporting the guests to sites around the island. We adopted this solution. One staircase was built for each stop. The truck driver and the assistant driver lifted each staircase into place when they arrived at the stop.

Staircase constructed for the 65th Anniversary Commemorating
the Battle of Iwo Jima

I wasn't the smartest person in the room. I couldn't come up with a solution no matter how hard I tried. Listening to and trusting in the knowledge of my engineering team was the key to our success. I keep this picture readily accessible on my computer to remind me that I am never so smart that I can't learn from those around me.

Conclusion

Plutarch wrote this about Alexander the Great:

[Alexander the Great] was naturally a great lover of all kinds of learning and reading;...When he was in the upper Asia, being destitute of other books, he ordered Harpalus to send him some; who furnished him with Philistus's History, a great many of the plays of Euripides, Sophocles, and Aeschylus, and some dithyrambic odes, composed by Telestes and Philoxenus.[4]

You don't know all of the situations you will face in your life. You don't know the future leadership positions you may hold, but you will be expected to be knowledgeable about your profession and the things that may affect it. Intelligence allows you to gather and process knowledge, the knowledge you may need to make better decisions in any leadership opportunity. No one wants to follow a leader they believe to be ignorant, so don't be. No matter how smart you become, don't let knowledge inflate your ego to the point where you stop learning from others around you.

Don't be *ignorant*. Be *intelligent*, but not *so intelligent that you become a know-it-all*. And *don't let your knowledge turn to pride*.

Food for Thought

Read this:

1. Read the autobiography of a famous leader. Does he or she mention the value of a library or books during the early formative years?
2. Start a reading program today. In order to ensure that you are obtaining both specific and general knowledge, consider a reading rotation. A reading rotation consists of selecting categories for reading and then rotating through each category. For example, make it your goal to read one book or magazine about your profession, followed by one book or magazine about a subject you want to know more about (current events, a hobby, biography, etc.),

followed by one that is purely for pleasure. Repeat the rotation. You'll always have something on hand to expand your knowledge base.

Watch this:

1. Think of something you have always wanted to know more about. Find a website with video lessons and get started.

Do this:

1. When was the last time you took a course? High school? College? Take a class in something today. Start with a course related to your field or industry and then take a class in something else you would like to learn—a language, music, and more. Just keep learning.

References

1. Proverbs 4:4–6.

2. Winston L. Spencer Churchill, *The Story of the Malakand Field Force: An Episode of Frontier War* (London: Longmans, Green, & Co., 1898), 283.

3. Andrew Carnegie, *Autobiography of Andrew Carnegie* (Boston: Houghton Mifflin Co., 1920), 182–83.

4. Plutarch, *The Lives of the Noble Grecians and Romans*, ed. Arthur Hugh Clough (New York: The Modern Library, 1864), 806.

Chapter 8

motivating
encouraging
cheerful positive

Enthusiastic

noun en·thu·si·asm \in-ˈthü-zē-ˌa-zəm, en-, also -ˈthyü-\
1
a : strong excitement of feeling : ardor • did her work with energy and enthusiasm
b : something inspiring zeal or fervor • his enthusiasms include sailing and fishing
2
a : belief in special revelations of the Holy Spirit
b : religious fanaticism

It's a Journey Together

If you ever wonder what enthusiasm looks like, spend time with children. Watch as they readily display excitement, disappointment, hope, and more excitement, all in a matter of minutes. They are the best barometers for enthusiasm as they are unencumbered and easily float from one feeling to another. As we grow up, we begin to calculate, worry about, and overthink the situations around us. Simple enthusiasm gets lost somewhere along the way, but we still know it when we see it. We know what brings us a smile, what encourages us, and what will make us go the extra mile.

Enthusiasm was never one of my strong traits. For years, I approached problems logically, creating my vision with the risks in mind so I could safely take my team from point A to point B. I was creative and ambitious when developing the vision, but the execution was all persistence and little enthusiasm. I was well suited to keep cadence for rowers in a Roman galley. "Shut up and keep rowing!" When I became a youth soccer coach, my methods were not effective. After learning from more experienced coaches, I started focusing on achieving and celebrating small victories, connecting them to the long-term goals and enjoying the journey as much as the destination. The teams I've worked with since then have been happier for it.

Whether the greatest challenge you face is static boredom or dynamic uncertainty, the ability to see a light at the end of the tunnel is a requirement for day-to-day survival. The ability to show the light is a requirement for leaders. We all want to be motivated, reassured, and encouraged as we contribute our effort into the team's work. We want to enjoy the journey that we're on together. Consider these extracts from the survey that relate to being enthusiastic. A leader is:

- someone who leads in a positive way and inspires confidence in others to follow
- a person with clear idea of the goal and how to reach it, while taking adequate precautions to prevent obstacles; but above all is able to motivate the others and utilise their best abilities
- a competent, caring team player who sees the big picture, translates it for others, and motivates his team to set and accomplish goals to achieve a common vision

- someone that is wise and knows what decisions to make to not only guide others, but also motivate and inspire others to reach their full potential
- a person who can motivate others to achieve a goal
- a person who motivates and inspires people to engage with a vision
- fair, goal oriented, motivated, motivates and leads those following, supportive, patient, understanding, understands that individuals matter too, knows when to step up and down as leader, and helps others that their leading
- the mover and shaker who motivates others towards the achievement of common goals motivating

---

You can understand a problem, develop and articulate a brilliant vision, and design a way forward to achieve your objectives. But if you can't enable and motivate people around you to give their best, you may fall short of your objectives, and you will fall short as a leader.

Mind Your Attitude

There is no disguising a lack of personal motivation. And everyone hates false enthusiasm. If you don't have it, you can't fake it. Loud greetings and oversized smiles are cause for suspicion. As King Solomon wrote:

If anyone loudly blesses their neighbor early in the morning, it will be taken as a curse.[1]

Who is *that* happy early in the morning? Before coffee? This same principle applies to any project you lead—don't fake it or overdo it. In the same way that compassion starts with you, real enthusiasm starts with you, too. If it is your project, you must find some element in it that genuinely motivates you. If you think there is nothing about it that is motivating, learn that every cloud has a silver lining. Find the silver lining, because that is your new home. While everyone else sees a big floating grey mass full of rain, you have to focus on the silver lining while managing the rain cloud—every day. It's easy to complain about what is difficult or why you can't do something. As a leader, you don't have that option anymore. If you honestly can't see a silver lining, make one. Find a way to add a purpose and a smile to whatever task you undertake.

The members of Sir Ernest Shackleton's crew were well-qualified to complain and give up their enthusiasm. Shackleton and his team set out to cross the Antarctic landmass. Upon arriving in Antarctica, his ship became stuck in the ice for an entire winter, later to be crushed by the shifting ice floes. The crew salvaged everything they could from the ship, including the life boats, and moved daily, searching for safe places to camp on the ice and eventually fleeing to Elephant Island. Over time, they realized that their only chance for survival was to attempt to sail a small boat to an island off South America that had a whaling station on it. While a small crew of six (Shackleton and five others) made the open boat journey through 800 miles of open ocean, the other 22 members of his crew had to wait on the barren Elephant Island, where they were exposed to incredibly high winds and little else. Shackleton and his small crew left on April 24. A rescue was successfully executed for the other 22 crewmen on August 30. The survival of that group for 128 days was attributed to Frank Wild, the person in charge of the group on Elephant Island:

> It is largely due to Wild, and to his energy, initiative, and resource, that the whole party kept cheerful all along, and, indeed, came out alive and so well. Assisted by the two surgeons, Drs. McIlroy and Macklin, he had ever a watchful eye for the health of each one. His cheery optimism never failed, even when food was very short and the prospect of relief seemed remote. Each one in his diary speaks with admiration of him. I think without doubt that all the party who were stranded on Elephant Island owe their lives to him. The demons of depression could find no foothold when he was around; and, not content with merely "telling," he was "doing" as much as, and very often more than, the rest. He showed wonderful capabilities of leadership and more than justified the absolute confidence that I placed in him.[2]

I would think that 17 months of Antarctic entrapment would take the enthusiasm out of almost anyone. Wild's endless supply of enthusiasm was credited with helping 21 others survive for the last four months in one of the most inhospitable environments on Earth. How is your supply of enthusiasm?

Shine for Others

Upon receiving their commissions as officers in the US Marine Corps, newly made second lieutenants attend a six-month training course known as The Basic School. There, we learned all manner of things—battlefield first aid, rifle and pistol marksmanship, land navigation, night operations, and so on. Good times! One of the exercises we conducted required us to navigate between four points on a map while leading 20 Marines. That was usually not a problem, but this was a night exercise. The night that had been chosen for our movement was overcast with heavy clouds. No moonlight or starlight hit the ground, and this was before night-vision goggles were common. I was one of two Marines in charge of this movement, which would also have hostiles in the form of other groups of Marine lieutenants stumbling around in the same section of East Virginia forests we would stumble through. So, navigate from A to B to C, and done at D; manage any hostile engagements with blank training rounds and don't get poked in the eye by a branch you can't see. Easy!

As we started out, it became immediately apparent that there would be no tactical spread between the members of our team. It was so dark, we ended up just grabbing the shoulder of the person in front of us while we all hoped the Marine in the front with a glow-in-the-dark compass could get us from A to B to C, and done. I was in the middle of the group, where I was supposed to help guide us through the night. It was slow going. About halfway to point C, someone behind me asked, "Where are we?" For whatever reason, my 22-year-old mind thought that was unnecessary chatter, so I said, "Just keep moving" (all persistence, no enthusiasm). The feedback I received at the end of the exercise was that I had not shared information that would have addressed concerns of others in the group. It would have been more helpful had I said, "We just passed B, and we'll be at C in 20 minutes." That piece of information would have helped everyone feel a little bit safer and happy to know we were on track as we stumbled through the woods on the darkest night of our lives. Instead, my answer made them feel like we were lost. A quick update was all that was needed to help everyone feel a little better.

Enthusiasm will affect your vocabulary—words you can or cannot use and how you say them. This may challenge your creativity, but words matter, especially when demonstrating enthusiasm. The good news is that practicing this skill is entertaining to yourself and to others. There is nothing better than creating your own style for responding to negative phrases, situations, and attacks against your team. I'm sure you've heard the term *bedside manner,* usually used in reference to doctors and nurses who have to talk to patients about sensitive subjects and diagnoses, some of which are chronic or fatal. Word choice is critical to how those professionals are perceived and how people receive the news that those professionals deliver. Plenty of people and groups will bring daily challenges to your progress. How you respond to that and keep a good attitude is a test of your enthusiasm.

Each negative statement you hear is an opportunity to exercise your "bedside manner" as a leader, shutting down attacks and negativity. You may also have heard the term *verbal sparring* where two or more people are jousting with words, trying to score a point against their opponent. When you are trying to maintain enthusiasm, you cannot spar or seek an argument. In the Marine Corps, we call this "verbal akido," usually used when a junior must spar with someone senior. Akido is a martial art in which all techniques are defensive and focus on using the aggressor's strength and size against them. In conversation, you are trying to turn a possible aggressive meaning away from your effort. In the case of enthusiasm, turning a negative to a positive (or at least a less negative) is the objective. WARNING: there may be a wonderful temptation to give a smart-aleck response. Try not to. Your goal is not to attack back, mount a staunch defense, or try to explain how wrong the other person is. Your goal is simply to deflect the negative statement away from you and the team and get back to the task at hand.

Write down things that people say to you that are meant to bring you down, and determine how much of their observation is valid and constructive. Then write down several possible responses you could give them that are *not* negative (or passive-aggressive). The next time someone attacks or criticizes you, use the phrases you've come up with to change a negative to a positive. Practice these until they become automatic. "I hadn't thought of that option." "Interesting. Let me think about it." "That is new information. Let me discuss it with ___ and get back to you." If you watch someone you respect as a leader, chances are they turn a phrase in this manner. If you have ever watched a skilled diplomat, they turn phrases to avoid negative areas. After all, our international relationships are important. Building bridges is a lot harder than burning them. Which one is happening in your conversations—building or burning? Take the challenge, start building bridges, relationships, and successful teams today. Put off the desire to take an easy shot when someone fires at you. Have a quiver of phrases that turn negatives to positives, or that at least redirect heat that comes at you and your team. And don't forget—how you say it is as important as what you say. If your words are happy and your face is angry, it doesn't count.

Simple Words

If someone has done something that is positive and observable, make sure you have these two words in your vocabulary: Thank you. There are few things that can put positive in the air as quickly as honest and sincere appreciation. There are many other simple words that should be in your vocabulary as you work with others. Learn the words that show courtesy and respect and model them for others. If you are working with an international team, this will require you to learn greetings and courtesies in another language. Your effort to do so will be noticed and appreciated. Your example will encourage others to show courtesy to their colleagues as well, creating a respectful environment every day.

Do everything you can to keep on track with your work and task. If you mess up, own it, and say it. There is nothing more negative than placing blame for your action (or inaction) onto someone else. If you do it once, your team will expect you to blame them in the future and will work hard to avoid being around you. If you can't put positive in the air, at least take the negative out. Just own the issue and focus on resolving the it. Remember, when the team makes a mistake, that is also something that you own. Don't let people get hung up on a setback. Own it, handle it, and move on. As always, there is too little and too much of this. Don't deflect blame onto others, and don't become a carpet for people to walk on, knowing that you'll let the dirt stick to you.

Don't underestimate the value of greetings, courtesies, thanks, and apologies and their impact on enthusiasm.

Conclusion

Enthusiasm can be seen in your presence and heard in your words as you express your thoughts. All of these things work together to inspire your colleagues. Enthusiasm works hand in hand with persistence to help you and the team move forward every day. As often as not, the goal of enthusiasm is to address and keep away the negative, rather than express only the positive. Find a way to move toward the vision, believe it is possible, and move forward every day. Getting closer to a goal motivates those around you and gives you the fuel to keep motivating. Enthusiasm can become self-sustaining with every small success you experience. Develop the vocabulary you need to respond to and deflect negative comments from your work and your team. Appreciate and enjoy the positive moments with those around you. You know you are moving forward, so don't let anyone hold you back physically or verbally. Enjoy moving forward with your team and make sure the team knows that you're glad to be a team.

Don't be *apathetic*. Be *enthusiastic*, but not so enthusiastic that *your cheerfulness is excessive*. And *never resort to false enthusiasm*.

Food for Thought

Read this:

1. Read *South! The Story of Shackleton's Last Expedition 1914–1917*. I'm not a big fan of the cold, so this tale was difficult to read. Find all the moments that the crew has an enthusiasm that you find hard to believe. It is an incredible tale of the effects of motivation on survival.

Watch this:

1. Type the word *enthusiasm* in a video search engine. How do people generate and keep enthusiasm?

Do this:

1. Start a list today of things people say to you that are discouraging or are meant to discourage you. Take the constructive parts of the input for action and think of a way to deflect the discouragement and write down your thoughts. Next to (or under) each phrase, write what you have heard others say in response to that phrase. Your achievement on the project, your recent and past performance, your knowledge of your team's abilities, and so on can all be fuel for making a positive statement. Put positive in the air every chance you get.

References

1. Proverbs 27:14.

2. Ernest Shackleton, *South! The Story of Shackletons Last Expedition 1914–1917* (The MacMillan Company, 1920), 240.

Chapter 9

Visionary

adjective vi·sion·ary \ˈvi-zhə-ˌner-ē\

1

: having or marked by foresight and imagination • a visionary leader • a visionary invention

2

a : of the nature of a vision : illusory

b : incapable of being realized or achieved : utopian • a visionary scheme

c : existing only in imagination : unreal

3

a : able or likely to see visions

b : disposed to reverie or imagining : dreamy

4

: of, relating to, or characterized by visions or the power of vision

No man exceeds Thomas A. Edison in broad vision and understanding. I met him first many years ago when I was with the Detroit Edison Company—probably about 1887 or thereabouts. The electrical men held a convention at Atlantic City, and Edison, as the leader in electrical science, made an address. I was then working on my gasoline engine, and most people, including all of my associates in the electrical company, had taken pains to tell me that time spent on a gasoline engine was time wasted—that the power of the future was to be electricity. These criticisms had not made any impression on me. I was working ahead with all my might. But being in the same room with Edison suggested to me that it would be a good idea to find out if the master of electricity thought it was going to be the only power in the future. . . .

At once he was interested. He is interested in every search for new knowledge. And then I asked him if he thought that there was a future for the internal combustion engine. He answered something in this fashion:

Yes, there is a big future for any light-weight engine that can develop a high horsepower and be self-contained. No one kind of motive power is ever going to do all the work of the country. We do not know what electricity can do, but I take for granted that it cannot do everything.

Keep on with your engine. If you can get what you are after, I can see a great future.[1]

—Henry Ford, *speaking of Thomas Edison*

The Skill You Are Already Practicing

Numerous people in the survey defined leadership with some variation of the word *vision*. Consider the following answers from the survey. A leader is:

- an honest person with a vision and ability to include and drive others towards the goal
- a leader has visionary ideas, persuade others to support these ideas and make them feel fulfillment in that process
- a pathfinder

- someone who can see the possibilities of future and paves the path for everyone to reach there
- a person with followers that believe and support a collective vision and mission that must be executed for the betterment of all who support and believe in the cause
- a person that has a vision and can lead an organization to achieve their goals
- a person with a vision
- a person with a vision who's energizing
- a visionary who inspires others
- sets a vision and creates a strategy to achieve specific goals
- showing the vision and value to be shared by a group of individuals
- someone who can see the future and take calculated risks by intuitive decisions

---

In your personal life, vision is the answer to these questions: What do I wish I had? What do I want to be? When applied to business projects or personal projects, vision is the answer to this question: What do I want it to look like when I'm done? There is immense value to knowing where you are and where you want to go. The right vision can motivate you and others to work hard to get from here to the future.

Before You Ask the Question

To answer the question "What do I want it to look like when I'm done?" you must understand what the situation looks like now. What is the problem? Take time to understand the problem. Where you are right now? What do you know? What do you wish you knew? What is going on?

The Wright brothers wrote that there are two ways to explore a problem:

Now, there are two ways of learning how to ride a fractious horse: one is to get on him and learn by actual practice how each motion and trick may be best met; the other is to sit on a fence and watch the beast awhile, and then retire to the house and at leisure figure out the best way of overcoming his jumps and kicks. The latter system is the safest; but the former, on the whole, turns out the larger proportion of good riders. It is very much the same in learning to ride a flying machine; if you are looking for perfect safety you will do well to sit on a fence and watch the birds; but if you really wish to learn you must mount a machine and become acquainted with its tricks by actual trial.[2]

It is hard to argue with their logic that experimentation and learning through trial and error produces true experts. Those persons most experienced in a field usually become the experts. But do not discount the value of watching for a while and then sitting and figuring out the best way of overcoming. Many problems we face have little cost when measured in time or money. In those problems, trial and error isn't prohibitively expensive, and you can rush right in. Other problems you face will have costs associated with trial and larger costs associated with error. The habit of pausing to observe and reflect can reduce risk and save you time and money as your projects become larger.

When I made paper airplanes as a child, I made all sorts of unfortunate experiments that were disappointing, to say the least. But the cost of that trial and learning was the cost of one piece of paper. When I flew sorties as a test pilot, an error during a test flight could damage the airplane or kill the pilot or aircrew onboard. For that reason, we conducted extensive aircraft testing on the ground to observe and detect areas of possible catastrophic failure, whether in wind tunnels or in the aircraft tied to the ground. Know when you're dealing with paper airplanes and when you're dealing with real ones. Are you playing with something very low cost that can't hurt you, or are you handling something larger, more expensive, and with potential risks for equipment and people? That can be your guide about how much time you spend observing and reflecting on the problem before you jump in to trial and error. Additionally, thinking about that can help you more judiciously allocate time and money to explore the problem before moving forward.

No matter the problem, there are elements outside of our control such as weather, personal injury, a shortfall of a critical resource, and more. It is tempting to see these unknowns and hesitate, seeking perfect clarity before taking even one step. Like we saw with the definition of traits, you can have too much or too little of anything, including clarity. Don't try to know it all. Be inquisitive and be aggressive as you look for details. Learn as much as you can, as quickly as you can, and then ask yourself this question: What do I want it to look like when I'm done? Remember also that part of your research into the question must be internal. Many problems have a moral element and, as mentioned in the chapter on courage, you have an internal decision to make when you face new problems. How you decide will directly impact how you move forward.

In the Department of Defense, teams are responsible for identifying the most important factors in a problem that must be addressed in the solution. They are called Key Performance Parameters, or KPPs, defined as follows:

> Performance attributes of a system considered critical to the development. . . .The number of KPPs identified. . .should be kept to a minimum to maintain program flexibility. Failure of a system to meet a validated KPP. . .brings the military utility of the associated system(s) into question, and may result in a reevaluation of the program or modification to production increments.[3]

Written in plain English, a short list of attributes must be present and measurable in the solution—lighter, cheaper, faster, stronger, whatever. What is the problem and what are the key attributes that you want the solution to have when you are done? Without the attributes you define, the solution generated will not solve the problem at hand. These parameters will help you choose a direction for your creative efforts as you develop your vision. Spending time understanding the problem is important.

Creating a Vision

What do you want it to look like when you're done?

Why do we ask, "Do you *see* what I mean?" Why do we call a plan a vision? The ability to construct an image of your current situation and, in your mind, reconstruct it into a better world is what makes someone a visionary. The ability to imagine a better situation is part of how we survive every day. When we are in a rut, an endless day-in and day-out cadence of repetitiveness, we tell ourselves that we are doing this for a better tomorrow. The vision that offers a better future inspires us to persist, one more day. Are you beginning a four-year college program? If you stick to it, you know you will earn a degree. Are you taking the first step of a marathon? Just take one step after another, and you can earn the pride of finishing. Is it the first day of your new diet and workout plan? Imagine how you will look and feel after months of sticking with it.

Visions keep us looking and moving forward. They give us a target to aim for, a direction for planning, something to focus on, and a reason to continue. If visions motivate us as individuals, what type of vision can motivate a group? What vision do you need to help people march alongside each other for a long journey? The idea of a better tomorrow may be defined differently by the members of your group. A unifying vision that brings people together is possible, and it is the responsibility of the leaders.

So what do you want it to look like when you are done? Answering that question is your opportunity to exercise creativity. It is also your opportunity to include the creativity of other members of the group when developing your way forward. Rarely is there only one answer to this question. That may happen when the matter deals with regulations or legalities that externally confine your options. At the other extreme, you sometimes have too many options to choose from. But in most cases, you have the latitude to choose from among many (but not too many) options. Researching the problem as a team and then creating a together vision is a key to building a vision that is attractive to everyone.

Some people take the first vision they see and start moving forward. Again, spending time understanding the problem is important so time spent developing the vision really addresses the problem. Creatively constructing the best vision is important so that planning toward your vision yields viable options that later enable you to make good decisions. Know that what you want may take time, that it may come step by step, and that the knowledge you amass along the way may be the key to enabling you to reach the final step of the vision.

Sharing the Vision

After examining the problem and developing your vision, you must communicate the vision to others. As discussed in the chapter on being articulate, simplicity is a great ally. When you answer the question, "What do you want it to look like when you are done?" less is more. Simultaneously, how you describe the vision is directly related to how you inspire others. The more colorful the vision, the easier it is to be charismatic when articulating it. In 1962, President John F. Kennedy voiced his vision of going to the moon:

> We choose to go to the moon. We choose to go to the moon in this decade and do the other things, not because they are easy, but because they are hard, because that goal will serve to organize and measure the best of our energies and skills, because that challenge is one that we are willing to accept, one we are unwilling to postpone, and one which we intend to win.[4]

Notice the use of tools discussed in the chapter on being articulate—the five Ws, inclusiveness, and confidence.

Each year, US Marine Corps units around the globe celebrate the birthday of the Marine Corps, November 10, 1775. It is typically a gala event for Marines, their spouses, and friends of the Marine Corps. On two occasions, I was the project officer in charge of designing the Birthday Ball. In each case, it would be a gala event for more than 600 guests. As with all gala events, funding was a key to its success. The fund I inherited for the first Birthday Ball had been thoroughly depleted and had to be investigated to ensure that no ethics rules had been violated in previous activities. With only two months to plan the event and with insufficient funds to start, I assembled a team and asked these questions so we could understand the problem at hand:

1. What are the external requirements for the event? The Marine Corps observes an order of events at the ball that must be followed by all units. Do we have the complete list on hand? Besides the external requirements, what requirements should we consider that are specific to this unit? (For example, we were an aviation unit located in Texas, so should we include something in the design that highlighted that?)
2. What do we want it to look like when we are done? Like all Marines, we wanted our ball to be the best, but what did *best* mean?

With these questions in mind, we began planning and identified the critical elements. Once we understood the problem, I gave them the vision:

1. The Birthday Ball must reflect well on us as a unit and as a military service while adhering to the requirements of the Marine Corps.
2. The event must be affordable for everyone in attendance (some birthday events have a ticket cost that is equal to approximately 10% of a junior Marine's paycheck).

Breaking it down into its most simple form, I gave them the KPPs, the simple description of what parameters must be in the solution:

professional + affordable

Focusing on just these two words, each team member took charge of their responsibilities. Those two words were the guides as the team members made decisions. When we met again, it was evident that everyone had tried to cut costs while making it a high-quality, professional event. Any vision you share should address the problem at hand, should be colorful or charismatic enough to interest others, and should break down into what Marines call the commander's intent, or simple answers to the question, "What do I want it to look like when we're done?"

Conclusion

The ability to generate the image of a better future, to communicate it to others, and then to move forward and make it happen are part of every leader's story. The basis of generating a better vision rests on a solid understanding of the situation you are currently facing. No leadership trait acts alone. The use of intelligence leads to understanding today, which leads to a vision for tomorrow. If someone comes into your office or your life and offers to fix all your problems with their idea, product, or service, beware! Watch to see if they immerse themselves in understanding your problem(s) first. Only from that understanding can anyone develop and project a vision for a better future. Charlatans and frauds skip the first step and offer prefabricated solutions before they really understand your situation. What is the problem? What do you want it to look like when you're done? Know the difference between a vision and hope. A vision is a desired outcome or a solution to a specific situation or problem. The vision is used as a basis for planning with the intent of achieving the goal. It requires work. Hope is a feeling or expectation for something to arrive in the future. Hope does not require action, just hope. A vision requires work.

Don't *just hope*. Be *visionary*, but not so visionary that *you forget what problem you're solving*. And don't *live only in your dreams—you have work to do*.

Food for Thought

Read this:

1. Who do you consider to be a real visionary today? There are numerous candidates you could consider: Elon Musk at SpaceX and Tesla; Bill and Melinda Gates at their foundation; CEOs of Google, Facebook, Amazon, and more. Many small businesses have visions that may be closer in size to what you are doing today. Start reading articles by these people, or follow them on networking sites. Where do you detect a vision? How do they articulate it? How can you emulate the behavior of these visionaries?

2. Read a news article about a problem. Get online and research it for five minutes. How would you describe the problem? What are the KPPs that must be addressed? What vision can you come up with that addresses the problem? That may seem difficult, but focus on understanding the problem and see what visions your understanding generates.

Watch this:

1. Watch an interview with the visionary you selected above. How do they talk about their own vision?

Do this:

1. At work, in your family, or on your sports team, decide what problem you are facing as a group. Spend some time learning the facts about the problem, defining KPPs, and putting priorities on the measures that you decide are critical. Afterward, answer the question, "What do I want it to look like when I'm done?" You may not be the boss, the head of family, or the coach, but develop a vision that meets the KPPs. Be creative and figure out a realistic, achievable vision and measures to know whether you have reached it.

2. Communicate the vision and KPPs you developed to your boss, your family, your coach, or your team. It doesn't matter if they embrace it or reject it—

just discuss the problem and vision with them. That's so you can practice the process of understanding the problem, developing KPPs, designing a vision, and articulating it, simply. If you are in a position to implement the vision, go for it!

References

1. Henry Ford, *My Life and Work* (New York: Doubleday, Page & Co., 1922), 234.

2. Wilbur and Orville Wright, *The Early History of the Airplane* (Dayton, OH; The Dayton-Wright Airplane Co, 1922), 16.

3. Joint Requirements Oversight Council, *Manual for the Operation of the Joint Capabilities Integration and Development System*, January 19, 2012, B-A-1.

4. John F. Kennedy, "John F. Kennedy Moon Speech," September 12, 1962, accessed January 15, 2018 at https://er.jsc.nasa.gov/seh/ricetalk.htm.

Chapter 10

Decisive

adjective de·ci·sive \di-'sī-siv\

1

: **having the power or quality of deciding** • The council president cast the decisive vote • a decisive battle

2

: **resolute, determined** • a decisive manner • decisive leaders • a decisive editor

3

: unmistakable, unquestionable • a decisive superiority

We, therefore, the Representatives of the United States of America, in General Congress, Assembled, appealing to the Supreme Judge of the world for the rectitude of our intentions, do, in the Name, and by Authority of the good People of these Colonies, solemnly publish and declare, That these united Colonies are, and of Right ought to be Free and Independent States, that they are Absolved from all Allegiance to the British Crown, and that all political connection between them and the State of Great Britain, is and ought to be totally dissolved; and that as Free and Independent States, they have full Power to levy War, conclude Peace, contract Alliances, establish Commerce, and to do all other Acts and Things which Independent States may of right do. — And for the support of this Declaration, with a firm reliance on the protection of Divine Providence, we mutually pledge to each other our Lives, our Fortunes, and our sacred Honor.[1]

—US Declaration of Independence,
a decision that changed the course of history

Decisions Have Impact

"What do you want to do tonight?"

"I don't know. What do you want to do?"

There are few things more frustrating than making plans with indecisive friends.

"You wanna get something to eat?"

"OK. What do you want to eat?"

"I don't know. What do you want to eat?"

Our actions are not accidental. We choose our actions. Our good intentions guide our decisions, but how many decisions turn out the results we envisioned? Some large and complex decisions have been made in the history of humankind, and we evaluate those decisions by studying their outcomes. Judging things that have already happened in the past is much easier than making decisions about the future. Given the importance of our decisions and their consequences, how we make decisions should be a focal point of academic study. Leaders have a greater obligation with their decisions because those decisions have consequences for a greater number of people.

How can someone prepare to make better decisions?

It was clear in the survey that people want to follow someone who can make a decision. It was also clear that decisiveness is closely linked to other leadership traits. According to the survey, a leader is:

- decisive, receptive and enabler of peoples' development
- one who looks after their team and makes the tough decisions
- the decision maker of the team
- a leader is someone that is wise and knows what decisions to make to not only guide others but also motivate and inspire others to reach their full potential
- a decisive visionary
- someone who makes decisions on behalf of a group and bears with the consequences
- the ability to make decisions and to influence and mobilize people
- someone who can see the future and take calculated risks by intuitive decisions
- someone you can trust to make the best choice no matter how hard the facts, yet shows mercy and kindness
- someone who makes the hard decisions but tries their best to do their fair share of the work too

---

One way to develop decisiveness is to have and to practice a procedure for decision making that can be used in every decision in your life. Problem-solving steps vary from source to source, but they generally have these same ingredients:

- Define and understand the problem
- Describe your desired outcome (vision)
- Determine or design ways to obtain your desired outcome
- Choose the best option
- Implement the decision

Just like traveling from one place to another, you ask, Where are you? Where do you want to be (your vision)? Which routes get you from one place to another? Choose the best path. Get moving.

How Many Ways Can You Get There from Here?

In the chapter on vision, you learned how to understand a problem and develop a vision of the desired outcome. Next, you must decide how to move forward. Every decision-maker values options—good, executable options. Military staff officers are challenged to develop at least three courses of action (COA) to accomplish any mission. Each course of action is fully developed and then presented for decision. In a way, developing three options when only one is needed may seem like a waste of effort. It is not. This process forces people to see the problem and the desired vision from different perspectives and creatively find unique ways to get from one to the other. It is like brainstorming, but the ideas are more fully developed than the list that brainstorming may generate. Whatever practice you embrace, brainstorming or COA development, it should encourage you to consider multiple, realistic options.

Challenge yourself to find different ways to achieve your vision.

One of the best ways to find different points of view is to enable your team members to generate the options. When my wife and I discuss going on vacation, we each generate different ideas. We often come up with very fun but very different options. In business, the solution from an engineering department probably won't look like one generated by a marketing department. No matter who is on your team, there will be a difference of opinion. Mixed teams come up with imaginative ways to move forward toward a common goal. The moment you think you are the only one who can find a way forward, you will be sacrificing service as a leadership trait. Respect the ability of those around you and solicit their ideas on how to move ahead. There is strength in diversity of thought, and the more varied the backgrounds of the people around you, the more varied the proposed solutions are likely to be.

Options are often restricted by two precious resources: time and capital. If you have only a little time, you must generate whatever option you can—*now*. If you have little capital (people, money, assets), you may have to generate options that can run on a shoestring budget, doing most of the work yourself. Knowing your assets before you begin is extremely important. There's no sense designing the Taj Mahal if you only have the budget, time, and manpower to set up a pup tent. Communicate all the constraints—space, time, weather, distance, budget—to everyone before you start generating options.

To ensure that only a reasonable number of options will be generated, look back to how you defined and understood the problem. In the chapter on vision, I mentioned a concept known as KPPs, or Key Performance Parameters. Each course of action that is designed and each idea that is the result of brainstorming must be measured against the list of KPPs. If the idea does not achieve the KPPs, the idea won't get you to your vision. Knowing the KPPs that are part of your task will help you design and select options that get you where you want to go. Also, they offer a concrete way to compare options once you have developed them.

Weighing the Options

Once you have developed a few realistic options, you'll need a way to compare them and make a final decision. By realistic, I mean something you can actually implement once you have made the decision. Often, people don't ask whether or not their ideas are realistic; that is, whether or not the resources required to implement the decision are on hand and what obstacles you will face once you get started. Once you have a list of realistic options, it's time to compare and decide.

In the previous example of the Marine Corps Birthday Ball, the two KPPs were "professional" and "affordable." At the event, it was customary to have a small gift in front of each place setting for people to take home as a souvenir of the evening. Here are the three options generated by our planning team:

Beer glass with unit emblem etched into the glass	$12
Two leather coasters with laser cut Marine Corps emblem	$ 2
Bottle opener embossed with Marine Corps emblem	$ 6

Since there was one gift per seat, the cost of the item would be directly added to each ticket price. We had a sample of each of the three gift options and could see that they were all professional in appearance and quality.

Which one did we choose to ensure that the event was affordable? At $2, the coasters were a clear winner. Each person received two coasters, and each couple received a total of four coasters. They were surprisingly high quality. The cost was low because they were locally produced.

NOTE: I received complaints from several people who wanted the beer glass. Remember, no choice you make will make everyone happy. Make the choice for what best supports your vision and move forward. In the end, the ticket price was $30 less than the previous year's celebration. All it took was a solid vision and a creative team. The event improved in quality and dropped in price.

Making a decision is difficult, but dealing with the consequences of a bad decision is much harder. As part of the process of making your decision, imagine what will happen to you in the next hours, days, or months after you decide. In the military, a process called wargaming is used, which actually makes two teams compete, role-playing through each course of action. Someone gets to play an adversarial role and highlight the probable areas of failure. You may not have the time and personnel on hand to do this, but you can play devil's advocate in your head. This role, originally *advocatus diaboli*, was allegedly used for centuries by the Catholic Church to argue against decisions being considered to ensure that all the facts on both sides of the argument had been discussed. If you have time to let someone play this role for you, take advantage of it. Having a living, thinking opponent will force you to consider things you hadn't, and may highlight areas of potential problems. If you don't have the time or don't have anyone you trust to take on this role, be prepared to do it yourself. My technique is to imagine the first three things I will have to accomplish if I choose option A and find the difficulties or hazards in those first steps before I embrace it too tightly. I have asked team members to do the same thing. What are the first three things you will need to accomplish to make this happen? That question has always generated a lot of thought and has identified a lot of hazards. Repeat this for each option you have developed.

Make the Decision

If you developed a clear vision and articulated it to the team, options generated by your team members are likely to be pretty realistic and usable. Don't be surprised if they become emotionally invested in their individual contributions. Despite this, a leader is expected to be decisive and make the final choice. Leaving it to democratic methods shows respect for your team and may put off some hurt feelings, but the leader is ultimately responsible for the right choice and the execution of that choice.

With this in mind, review the KPPs for each of the options you and your team have made and select one of the following:

- Choose one of the courses of action
- Develop a course of action based on the best parts of each proposal
- Discard the options if they fail to achieve the vision or solve the problem at hand

Don't drag out the work of asking for more research within the options unless additional information has become available or the options presented don't achieve the objective. If one (or both) of the options gets you where the team needs to be, *make a decision* and get started.

Remember that not all KPPs are equal. Some factors are more important than others. Know what the highest priority is. If two options address all the KPPs, you can choose the one that more thoroughly addresses the highest priority KPP. In the example I have been using, having a professional event was more important than having an affordable event. I could not sacrifice our adherence to professional requirements just to save a few more dollars.

WARNING: Remain adaptable to changes that may happen on the way or lessons that may be learned as everyone gets to work. As discussed in the chapter on vision, if your plan achieves the objective and something can be added that is cheap and easy *and* improves the final product, then incorporate it. If you are on track to your objective and something can be added that is expensive and difficult and *might* improve the final product, then skip it and move on. Written briefly, better can be "free for the taking" or better can be the enemy of "good enough." As a leader, it is your role to know which type of change you're looking at.

Conclusion

Good intentions and great hopes are rarely the ingredients for approaching a decision with respect to its long-term impact. At the end of World War I, the Allied Powers gathered to create the Treaty of Versailles to determine how to return to life after war. John Maynard Keynes, a famous economist, analyzed the finished treaty. He later wrote a book, *The Economic Consequences of the Peace*, discussing its probable impact. He wrote:

> This chapter must be one of pessimism. The Treaty includes no provisions for the economic rehabilitation of Europe,—nothing to make the defeated Central Empires into good neighbours, nothing to stabilise the new States of Europe, nothing to reclaim Russia; nor does it promote in any way a compact of economic solidarity amongst the Allies themselves; no arrangement was reached at Paris for restoring the disordered finances of France and Italy, or to adjust the systems of the Old World and the New.[2]

Many, like Keynes, would see that the treaty was a decision to inflict punishment instead of a decision to enable continental peace. The unintended consequence of this decision was a second World War only 20 years later.

The vision you create should be thorough and conform with what you truly believe must be done for the long term. The process that brings you to a decision should address the KPPs of your vision that ensure what is most valuable to the outcome. Consider all the necessary factors and make the best decision you can. Make your decision with its consequences in mind.

Once you have made your decision, get the word out. With an articulate instruction or speech, let the team know what problem we are addressing, where we're going (vision), and how we'll get there. Then get started! At this point, decisiveness gives way to persistence as you make daily progress toward your goal. Courage helps you face challenges to your choices, even when things get tough. Moral courage also gives you the integrity to stay true to the intent of your vision even when easy, but questionable, options become available. Enthusiasm sustains the team throughout.

The decision is the end of one process and the beginning of another. While you must continue to observe and reflect on the things you learn while you move forward, there is rarely any benefit in turning back once you've made the decision. Integrate new information as you go, adjust course if you must, but keep moving forward. In the case of a very long project, pause occasionally to review the steps you have taken. This is especially true if a large number of people on your team have left and new people have come onboard. Take the time to show them how you got here: problem, vision, decision, and work to date. Then get moving again.

Don't be *wishy-washy*. Be *decisive*, but not so decisive that *you make decisions too hastily*. And never *fail to consider the consequences of your decisions.*

Food for Thought

Read this:

1. What document do you believe most significantly changed the course of history? For that document, find a book or story about the meetings, conferences, or convention *behind* the decision. Do you see a discussion of problems? Who articulates a vision? How was the decision really made?

Watch this:

1. Type the word *decisive* into an internet search engine. What videos come up? Watch one and see what you think. Is it relevant or not?

Do this:

1. What is the next decision you are going to make? Pay close attention because you make them all the time. Observe closely how you are making decisions and if you have a process. Do you identify the key areas of importance? If so, do you take them into consideration when you decide, or do you go with what is easy? Slow down and observe your current process. Is there room for improvement?

2. In the previous chapter, you were encouraged to find a news article, evaluate the problem, and create a vision. Using the same article, generate options and decide what you would do. Test your decision by deciding this: What are the first three things you would do now that you've decided? Is it still realistic? Consequences matter. If you can't follow up your decision with action, back up and reevaluate the problem, the vision, and the decision.

References

1. "The Declaration of Independence." *USHistory.org*, accessed January 15, 2018, at http://www.ushistory.org/declaration/document/.

2. John Maynard Keynes, *The Economic Consequences of the Peace* (London: MacMillan and Co., 1920), 211.

Chapter 11

Persistent

adjective per·sis·tent \pər-ˈsi-stənt, -ˈzi-\

1

: existing for a long or longer than usual time or continuously: such as

a : retained beyond the usual period • a persistent leaf

b : continuing without change in function or structure • persistent gills

c : effective in the open for an appreciable time usually through slow volatilizing • mustard gas is persistent

d : degraded only slowly by the environment • persistent pesticides

e : remaining infective for a relatively long time in a vector after an initial period of incubation • persistent viruses

2

a : continuing or inclined to persist in a course

b : continuing to exist despite interference or treatment • a persistent cough • has been in a persistent vegetative state for two years

How to Get from Here to There

Students are often encouraged to join clubs so they can pursue their passions outside the classroom and meet others with the same interests. An MBA program is no different. Our class was encouraged to form an Entrepreneur Club, a Finance Club, a Consulting Club, and so on. As a formerly certified personal trainer, I decided to form a club for exercise, since sitting at a desk for eight hours a day hardly fostered health and well-being. Not too many people signed up. Of those who did, several came only once, a few attended regularly, and one attended almost every session. That individual continued to exercise consistently after the MBA program was concluded. The result of his persistence was a loss of 22 pounds (10 kilograms) of body weight over an eight-month period. He looked great, felt great, and was healthier overall. Persistence paid off. Like other traits of leadership, persistence has a few key elements and it doesn't work alone.

Let's look now at the survey responses that point to persistence. A leader is:

- a person of strong will and determination
- a person who helps the team to get to its goals
- a person with a vision and commitment to make that vision a reality
- driven
- getting stuff done
- someone you can follow or you can rely on
- the person others count on to drive a successful conclusion
- a person with a vision and the commitment to see it through by engaging the people around her
- a person that delivers result thru drive, empathy, and passion

---

Like other traits, persistence can be learned, practiced, and improved. While all of the "need to know" elements of leadership are important, doing them only once in your life isn't enough to become a leader. Having the persistence to demonstrate these traits every day is a key to becoming a better leader. Like the benefits of physical exercise, the character traits of leadership aren't visible and don't last long without persistence to keep you going and growing.

Put One Foot in Front of the Other

Booker T. Washington dedicated his life to service-based leadership aimed at providing education and opportunity for African-Americans after the US Civil War. He was constantly working to improve conditions for those around him, including his attempt to expand the trade school in Tuskegee, Alabama:

I had always supposed that brickmaking was very simple, but I soon found out by bitter experience that it required special skill and knowledge, particularly in the burning of the bricks. After a good deal of effort we moulded about twenty-five thousand bricks, and put them into a kiln to be burned. This kiln turned out to be a failure, because it was not properly constructed or properly burned. We began at once, however, on a second kiln. This, for some reason, also proved a failure. The failure of this kiln made it still more difficult to get the students to take any part in the work. Several of the teachers, however, who had been trained in the industries at Hampton, volunteered their services, and in some way we succeeded in getting a third kiln ready for burning. The burning of a kiln required about a week. Toward the latter part of the week, when it seemed as if we were going to have a good many thousand bricks in a few hours, in the middle of the night the kiln fell. For the third time we had failed.

The failure of this last kiln left me without a single dollar with which to make another experiment. Most of the teachers advised the abandoning of the effort to make bricks. In the midst of my troubles I thought of a watch which had come into my possession years before. I took this watch to the city of Montgomery, which was not far distant, and placed it in a pawn-shop. I secured cash upon it to the amount of fifteen dollars, with which to renew the brickmaking experiment. I returned to Tuskegee, and, with the help of the fifteen dollars, rallied our rather demoralized and discouraged forces and began a fourth attempt to make bricks. This time, I am glad to say, we were successful. Before I got hold of any money, the time-limit on my watch had expired, and I have never seen it since; but I have never regretted the loss of it.

Brickmaking has now become such an important industry at the school that last season our students manufactured twelve hundred thousand of first-class bricks, of a quality suitable to be sold in any market.[1]

It took Washington four tries to successfully make a brick oven for students at the trade school, but his persistence paid off, and 1.2 million bricks were made the year he wrote the book. Success came at personal cost, but it paved the way for training hundreds of students in a valuable trade, and it created an additional funding source for the school. Persistence in the face of repeated failure took courage and a strong belief in his mission to serve the students of that institute.

Persistence doesn't always mean moving forward in the face of intense adversity or failure. With the courage to overcome, you can move forward if you are persistent through failure and difficulty. But not every task you face requires extreme courage, and not every action will be recorded in the history books. Patience is persistence in a moment when there is no action to take. Sometimes persistence simply means moving forward. In sport highlights, we always see the game-changing moments and incredible plays, but the two-minute summary of the week's sporting events are only a few moments among tens of thousands of decisions, actions, moves, plays, and attempts that were not shown. There is power in realizing that the unrecorded moments caused the highlight moments. Sometimes, the only action you can take is that of stepping on the field and playing to the best of your ability. It might not be courageous. You might not be faced with tough decisions. You may not appear in the highlight reel on the news. You just have to play.

Some days are drudgery. Some of the things we do are repetitive, and we don't think they lead anywhere. But when persistence is applied in the direction of a vision, you will find moments where you break through, leap forward, and eventually arrive at your destination.

Marie Curie dedicated herself to a life of research and discovery. She progressed by working every day in her chosen scientific field. After years of research, she was on a team of three people who were awarded a Nobel Prize in Physics. After receiving the most esteemed scientific prize, she persisted in her research, even after her husband (and research partner) had passed away and she was raising children as a single parent. Her persistence led to more discovery and a second Nobel Prize (this time in Chemistry) in 1911, eight years after the first. Persistence made her the first scientist to receive two Nobel Prizes in Science.

In the case of Mahatma Gandhi, there were 25 years between the publication of his pamphlet on Home Rule (or self-rule, independence) and India's eventual independence. His goal was clear, but it was a marathon effort of day-by-day, step-by-step efforts. Gandhi is the most famous name among those who made these efforts, but the day-in, day-out activities of countless people were required. Among those infinite actions, there were moments of adversity and moments of victory that resulted in steps toward the vision that Gandhi wrote about in 1922.

Similarly, Nelson Mandela joined the African National Congress (ANC) and the fight for equality in South Africa in 1944. It wasn't until 1994—50 years later—that South Africa held its first multi-racial democratic election. Those 50 years took Mandela through protest, 27 years in prison, an election campaign, and the difficult job of uniting South Africa. When a vision is so great, persistence through a long-term goal can seem impossible. Fifty years can seem like an eternity. It's more than half of an average lifetime. So how do you keep moving forward, day after day, for so long? How do you encourage others to keep moving forward with you?

Breaking Down the Journey into Individual Steps

The US military teaches its officers a problem-solving methodology on how to approach large problems. In that process, there is a step in which everyone is told to analyze the mission to discover the smaller pieces of the job that need to be completed. In other words, break down the big job into little jobs.

Here is an example of a mission that anyone may face some day: Host a birthday party for a child.

This may sound simple, but there is more to it than meets the eye. Service members are taught to look for individual tasks that are *specified* by the mission and those that are *implied* by the mission. A specified task is one that is legible in the mission statement. (If you work at a company, specified tasks may also appear in policy documents or memoranda that dictate how some actions must be taken on behalf of the company.) In the mission above, it's specified that we need to have a party. An implied task is defined by the US Marine Corps as:

> not specifically stated in the. . .order, but they are necessary to accomplish specified tasks. Implied tasks emerge from analysis of the. . .order, the impending threat, and the understanding of the problem.[2]

Implied tasks for this mission are those that appear as we consider subordinate tasks or areas of possible threat:

- Who will be on the guest list?
- Do we need invitations? What kind? Paper or e-vites?
- Is there a theme for the party? What does the child like?
- Do we need a meal, a birthday cake, or both? Does anyone have any allergies?
- Where will we have the party?

You can probably think of a few more to add. As you break down the primary task—birthday party—smaller tasks appear that may seem more manageable and even fall into a natural order. For example, it may be smart to know the theme of the party and how many people are attending *before* you design the invitations, choose the location, or order the cake and other food.

While this is a simple example, the principle applies to all large problems as well. Breaking down the long-term purpose of your actions can help you find small steps that get you where you want to go. This is a key to persistence. Know the vision and the work you need to accomplish, break it down into small, realistic tasks (small steps), get started, and keep moving.

Helping Others Persist

The process above is also the key to incorporate others into your efforts. Once you have determined the smaller tasks that must be accomplished, you may have an idea of who to recruit or whose help you'll need to accomplish the tasks. In the case of my son's most recent birthday party, my daughter knew what kind of cake he would like. She took charge of buying it and choosing the design. He really liked the cake, and she was very happy to have helped.

As others begin to accomplish the small tasks that add up to the big task, you have a unique opportunity to do something that helps everyone on the team stick to the task. Celebrate! When someone on the team accomplishes one of the tasks, make sure the team knows what was done and who did it. This is also a time to reiterate what the team is doing, what is next, why they are doing it, and what it will look like when they are done. The ability to celebrate the accomplishments of those around you requires enthusiasm as well as the willingness to appreciate how important everyone on your team is (think: compassion and service). Like a connect-the-dots puzzle, you can begin to see the shape of the final effort once a few of the lines are drawn. The ability to see that your efforts are leading to something bigger is what keeps the pencil moving in such a puzzle, and it is also what keeps people moving when involved in a long-term project.

WARNING: There can be an excess of celebration. There comes a time when acknowledgments and rewards become so common and so expected that they cease to mean anything. A generic acknowledgment of someone's effort isn't an acknowledgment. Likewise, not everything deserves a party. There can be *too little* and *too much*.

Conclusion

"How do you eat a whale?"

It's the classic question asked of anyone facing a large project.

The answer: "One bite at a time."

"What is the most important play in the game?"

The answer: "The next one."

Get moving, keep moving, and be prepared to continue forward for much longer than you think. Booker T. Washington didn't give up with three attempts. He believed it was necessary to build a brick kiln, and it didn't happen until the fourth try. Marie Curie didn't stop her search for knowledge when she was awarded the highest prize known for science because there was more to discover. Neither Gandhi nor Mandela stopped when they reached their goals. Consider Nelson Mandela's farewell address that he gave after his presidency, 55 years after joining a political party:

> Today we start the ultimate session of our first democratic parliament. The pro-found changes of the past four-and-half years make the distance traversed seem so short; the end so sudden. Yet with the epoch-making progress that has been made, this period could have been decades. South Africa is in a momentous process of change, blazing a trail towards a secure future. The time is yet to come for farewells, as many of us—by choice or circumstance—will not return. However, there is no time to pause. The long walk is not yet over. The prize of a better life has yet to be won.[3]

After 55 years, the long walk was not over. Celebrate what you have accomplished, but persist in moving forward—every day.

Don't *give up*. Be *persistent*, but not so persistent that *you can't stop and appreciate the distance you've come*. And don't *forget to appreciate others who make it possible*.

Food for Thought

Read this:

1. What was the longest effort made by a single person that you can think of? Careful! The examples above are significant, but see if you can find a story of someone who dedicated their entire life to one vision. Who was it, and why did they do it?

Watch this:

1. A web search for an acceptance speech will yield both the video and the text of various persons accepting a wide variety of acknowledgments and prizes. Watch an acceptance speech to see where and how persistence appeared as an ingredient of success.

Do this:

1. It is time to set a goal that cannot be achieved in one day. Examples include education, physical wellness, or developing a new skill. Make a vision that addresses a problem you face. Research the options and become knowledgeable of ways you can move toward this new goal. Then decide and get going. Schedule the progress you want to see by selecting intermediate tasks and goals. Take action daily to reach this new goal, and stick to the plan. There is no other way to practice persistence.

References

1. Booker T. Washington, *Up from Slavery* (New York: A.L. Burt Co., 1901), 151–152.

2. US Marine Corps. *Marine Corps Planning Process.* August 24, 2010, accessed January 15, 2018, at https://www.mca-marines.org/files/MCWP%205-1%20MCPP.pdf.

3. Nelson Mandela, "Address by President Nelson Mandela to Parliament National Assembly, Cape Town," 5 February 1999, accessed January 15, 2018, at http://www.mandela.gov.za/mandela_speeches/1999/990205_sona.htm.

Chapter 12

Courageous

noun cour·age \\'kər-ij, 'kə-rij\\
mental or moral strength to venture, persevere, and withstand danger, fear, or difficulty

What Cannot Be Begun Cannot Be Finished

Modern versions of courage are often defined by images provided by Hollywood. Many movies celebrate the bold and visible forms of courage in action thrillers, stories from war, and so on. Some movies also portray moments of quiet courage, or courage that thinks and acts but doesn't necessarily wrestle physically with a visible enemy. For many of us, courage is simply the will to go on when we are unsure or afraid. It does not require words or brave deeds but only the actions of everyday living in uncertain or frightening conditions. In any of these examples, you are witnessing a specific process—the willingness to move from a belief to an action. Courage is the trait that underlies the process.

Like leadership, we know courage when we see it, but that hardly tells us how to become more courageous as individuals. The chapter on traits contains various quotes on courage from Wu Tzu and Aristotle. Courage was woven into all the stories of past leaders and still features in the survey definitions of leadership. The definition of courage at the beginning of the chapter is from Merriam-Webster. It begins with "mental or moral strength." According to the answers from the survey, a leader is:

- somebody who is conscientious, courageous and caring
- courageous
- bold
- courage
- leading from the front, involved in employee development, owns mistakes of the team, accounts on behalf of the team, is visionary and goal oriented, never apportions blame but assists in resolving issues. Courageous and assertive, strategic and a certain level of charisma.
- someone who does the right thing

Napoleon's *Maxims of War*, a collection of his observations as a commander, highlights an interesting facet of courage.

MAXIM XVIII.

A general of ordinary talent occupying a bad position, and surprised by a superior force, seeks his safety in retreat; but a great captain supplies all deficiencies by his courage, and marches boldly to meet the attack. By this means he disconcerts his adversary; and if the latter shows any irresolution in his movements, a skillful leader, profiting by his indecision, may even hope for victory, or at least employ the day in maneuvering—at night he entrenches himself, or falls back to a better position. By this determined conduct he maintains the honor of his arms, the first essential to all military superiority.[1]

In Napoleon's words, courage "supplies all deficiencies." While he and several other French generals may have attributed too much capability to courage, they were right to say that when other resources are lacking, courage can enable and sustain efforts until the situation changes.

Courage is a trait, and we know it when we see it. But it is not just the action itself, or what we see. The visible act of courage is the final phase. Courage begins in deeply rooted belief, becomes a decision, and then turns into action.

Becoming Courageous

A strong, deeply rooted belief in right and wrong causes people to speak when they might not and act when they otherwise would not. It sets their standards for telling the truth, keeping promises, and accomplishing many virtuous acts. A sense of right and wrong can come from many sources. Among the leaders named by survey participants, religious founders and religious personages were named. They included Mother Teresa, Pope Francis, the Prophet Muhammad, and Joan of Arc. Religion often provides a sense of right and wrong. A sense of right and wrong can also come from ideologies such as democracy, socialism, or communism. Other "isms"—capitalism, altruism, feminism, and so on—give people a direction and a sense of justice. Culture plays a role as well. We were taught social rights and wrongs by those around us when we were growing up. (Note: these cultural points are "nice to know" when you work with internationally diverse groups).

Experience also plays a role in what we believe is right or wrong. This is the case for long-standing beliefs or workplace habits that are formed at jobs.

"We've always done it this way" is a deeply rooted belief that gives people a sense of safety. "We've tried that before, and it didn't work" expresses a fear of failure and may prevent people from trying something new. "This works every time" gives people a sense of confidence that will encourage them to move ahead. But experience is a double-edged sword that can bring problems as well as solutions. Allow me to paraphrase a saying among Marines that gives a humorous warning about basing decisions on professional experience.

> There are three things you never want to hear:
> a lieutenant say, "In my experience. . ." or
> a captain say, "Watch this. . ." or
> a major say, "I have a great idea."

The reasons are that a lieutenant is the most junior officer and has no experience; a captain has experience, but not enough to know all of the hazards of the business, so "watch this" really means "watch out!"; and a major has experience, but for a major, it's best to come up with the idea and then have someone else do the work.

Religions, ideologies, cultures, and experience all contribute to a person's sense of right and wrong. Understanding your own beliefs is the first step to developing courage.

It is important to know what others in the group or organization think as well. There are times when your willingness to act on your convictions will galvanize a group, but there are also times when your beliefs may be divisive. Knowing the source of your own beliefs, as well as those of the people around you, can help you see three large categories into which your words and actions will fall.

> When you and others will agree about what is right.
> When you and others neither agree nor disagree but are willing to act together.
> When you and others disagree about what is right.

Agreement is more easily reached among people with similar backgrounds and beliefs, especially when they have worked together for a long time. Conversely, diverse groups of people who are newly introduced will have more sources of possible disagreement. These disagreements are natural, are something everyone will face, and are nothing to be afraid of.

Understanding your beliefs and why you believe them is the first step to acting with courage. These beliefs motivate you to make decisions and take action. Everyone's willingness to act will come from their "mental or moral strength to. . .persevere," as stated in the definition. If you are working on something you believe to be wrong, you are unlikely to support the effort with your whole strength. By identifying everyone's beliefs, vested interests, or cultural foundations, you can understand in advance how your decisions may be received by the group and what you'll need to do to move beyond any disagreement. This will enable you to see when tough situations may arise and what kind of courage you'll need to face them.

What Is a Courageous Decision?

It is not uncommon for people to mask their ideas of right and wrong. This is done out of fear of persecution, fear of offending others, or other feelings of uncertainty. Everyone has some idea in their minds of what is right and wrong. Your sense of right and wrong heavily affects how you make decisions and how you treat others. Here, courage overlaps with decisiveness and compassion, covered previously in this book.

There is fear in many everyday decisions. Resources can only be spent once. You may make an unpopular decision. You may be wrong. Overcoming fear is an internal process. Collect the facts, determine all options available to you, and then decide what you think is right for this situation. Some groups decide democratically, but that is not leadership. That is governance or facilitation, but not leadership. Leadership is making the decision, even when you are responsible for consequences you may not like. Deferring to a group vote can be an attempt to pardon yourself from suffering the consequences of unpopularity or of being wrong. It gives you excuses ("You all chose this, not me"). A courageous act is one you do even though the consequences may be fatal to your career, your reputation, or your life. Deferring to the popular vote is side-stepping an opportunity to be courageous. Does this mean that democratic decision-making is wrong? No, it has a time and a place. Concepts such as "the consent of the governed" are important in decisions that will affect everyone equally, such as the ideas championed by Susan B. Anthony.

It is often the case that those in positions of leadership have access to more information than everyone else. That information may force leaders toward a decision that will be unpopular in the short term until others learn the same facts. Convictions of right and wrong are part of what allow you to decide and focus on longer-term outcomes. Notice that in the previous section, many of the sources of right and wrong are long-term concepts. That is, their sources have implications far down the road (even eternity), tying courage with vision. This long-term belief sustains individuals through short-term difficulties.

An internal decision based on your sense of right and wrong is a key to courage. If your decision is based on a desire to be popular, a short-term gain, or an easy opinion, then it doesn't require too much courage. Knowing what is right, choosing that path, and moving ahead regardless of what others think is the way of courage.

For many years as a Marine, I had to complete the semi-annual physical fitness test: pull-ups, sit-ups, and a three-mile run. During one fitness test, I was to conduct the test with only one other officer. That required a non-participating officer to witness and verify the scores. These tests had an impact on promotions, so it could be uncomfortable if you are counting pull-ups or sit-ups for another Marine and they perform poorly. At 0600, I reported to the sports field. I was first up for pull-ups and did 18 in accordance with the regulations. Not a perfect score, but not bad. The other Marine jumped up and started in good form, but after 10 or so, his form began to give, and after 16, he was not able to make it up to the bar. He tried twice more to get his chin over the bar, but didn't quite make it. He dropped from the bar and shook his head. I told him I had counted 16. He asked me to write 18 on the score card.

What do you do?

What if I tell you that this officer was a higher rank than I was? What if I told you that this officer was responsible for writing my performance evaluation that year? What do you do? That was a cold November morning but it felt colder as he looked at me and directed me to write the number

18. I believed it was wrong. I decided I would not write 18, and I told him so. He took the scorecard and prepared to write it himself when the witness, also junior to the officer in question, stepped forward and stated that he would not sign as a witness if the number 18 was written as his score. The witness and I both knew that what we believed was right. We made an internal decision, and we stated our decision.

Translating Thought into Action

When you have made a decision based on what you believe to be right, putting the decision into words is often the first thing a leader must do. The chapter on vision and decisiveness talk about including the information and opinions of others into your decision-making. Still, choosing among competing options takes courage, and the leader must decide. Communicating the decision to others is aided by being articulate, but the real difficulty is in overcoming fears associated with consequences of the decision. When you speak, your thought processes are laid bare for all to see. Also, when you speak, you may face unpleasant consequences. A belief of doing right protects you from negative feedback of this nature.

When you announce your decision, it may meet opposition immediately. As discussed in the chapter on compassion, the opinions of those around you deserve consideration. For good reason, you may modify your decision as you move forward. Your team members' intuitions and input are valuable. But the longer you work at one project, the more opinions emerge. Integrity is having the courage to stay on course despite the challenges that tempt you to submit to opinions or conditions around you. Persistence is continuing forward, despite friction or challenges that arise in your path. Many leaders named in the survey faced overwhelming odds as they achieved their life's work. Some of them were Dr. Martin Luther King, Jr., Mahatma Gandhi, Harriet Tubman, Mustafa Kemal Atatürk, Abraham Lincoln, and many more. A deeply rooted belief in the rightness of your action helps you persist and gives you the integrity to remain faithful to your intent.

Courage can be learned. Consider the quote below from Theodore Roosevelt. A sickly boy, he became a cowboy, a police commissioner, an officer in a military unit, a US president, a Nobel Peace Prize recipient, a recipient of the US Congressional Medal of Honor, and many other things. Working his way up in New York politics was an unsafe business. Consider this account from his time as a committee chairman in the New York Assembly. He knew he should get the bill out of committee and introduce it to the floor, but he also knew there were corrupt congressmen (called the "combine") on his committee who wanted to prevent it from advancing:

> There was a broken chair in the room, and I got a leg of it loose and put it down beside me where it was not visible, but where I might get at it in a hurry if necessary. I moved that the bill be reported favorably. This was voted down without debate by the "combine," some of whom kept a wooden stolidity of look, while others leered at me with sneering insolence. I then moved that it be reported unfavorably, and again the motion was voted down by the same majority and in the same fashion. I then put the bill in my pocket and announced that I would report it anyhow. This almost precipitated a riot, especially when I explained, in answer to statements that my conduct would be exposed on the floor of the Legislature, that in that case I should give the Legislature the reasons why I suspected that the men holding up all report of the bill were holding it up for purposes of blackmail. The riot did not come off; partly, I think, because the opportune production of the chair-leg had a sedative effect, and partly owing to wise counsels from one or two of my opponents.[2]

It was a bold move to bring a chair leg, for use as a club, into a congressional committee meeting, but he believed there was corruption among the committee members, and he was determined to advance the cause, regardless. He knew what he believed to be right. He decided to act upon that belief, and he *planned ahead*. In his own words, courage was not a trait he was born with:

> There were all kinds of things of which I was afraid at first, ranging from grizzly bears to "mean" horses and gun-fighters; but by acting as if I was not afraid I gradually ceased to be afraid. Most men can have the same experience if they choose. They will first learn to bear themselves well in trials which they anticipate and which they school themselves in advance to meet. After a while the habit will grow on them, and they will behave well in sudden and unexpected emergencies which come upon them unawares.
>
> It is of course much pleasanter if one is naturally fearless, and I envy and respect the men who are naturally fearless. But it is a good thing to remember

that the man who does not enjoy this advantage can nevertheless stand beside the man who does, and can do his duty with the like efficiency, if he chooses to.[3]

In his description of how to develop courage, he addressed the question about whether courage can be learned or if you're just born with it. For some, it is a matter of practice. By preparing in advance for known, anticipated situations, you can grow courage. This can be as simple as preparing to ask someone a yes or no question. Their answer will either be yes, or it will be no. What will you do if they say yes? What will you do if they say no? Preparing for a scenario of limited possible outcomes is one way to plan ahead and maintain your calm and courage during a difficult situation. Planning lets you act in a way that is unafraid. You have anticipated what could happen and you have prepared. Repetitive training can also prepare you for courageous action. First responders such as firefighters, police officers, and emergency medical technicians face dangerous situations in a courageous manner, partly because they have trained repeatedly to do so.

A test pilot is expected to go outside of the comfort zone known for aircraft. To do this, a dozen hours (or more) are put into planning before any one hour of flight or test operation is conducted. Why? To prepare everyone to face a potentially dangerous or frightening situation with courage and to execute the test. To consider all the possible outcomes and what actions the team will take for each one. Just like Theodore Roosevelt recommended, everyone is prepared to meet a situation, to act in a courageous manner, and to succeed.

Deciding beforehand how you will meet a situation will help you plan, prepare, and then behave in a manner that is steadfast and courageous. Notice that Roosevelt started with frightening situations with animals. That implies that it may be better *not* to make the corporate boardroom your first test of this theory. Start small. Easier circumstances often arise between friends, and you can practice there. Note that the goal of this practice isn't to win. The goal is to focus on and improve your ability to maintain composure in situations that unnerve or frighten you. Practicing this skill enough can make it natural, like any learned skill.

It's worth noting that Roosevelt went on to write that he envied those "who are naturally fearless." For some, there are leadership traits that are more natural or that are learned at a very young age, making them seem innate. Regardless of how you measure yourself in any of these leadership traits or as a leader, there is always a way to improve.

Conclusion

Inazo Nitobé was a Japanese scholar whose book describes the Japanese honor code known as Bushido. In it, he connected courage to honorable beliefs.

> Courage was scarcely deemed worthy to be counted among virtues, unless it was exercised in the cause of Righteousness. In his "Analects" Confucius defines Courage by explaining, as is often his wont, what its negative is. "Perceiving what is right," he says, "and doing it not, argues lack of courage." Put this epigram into a positive statement, and it runs, "Courage is doing what is right." To run all kinds of hazards, to jeopardize one's self, to rush into the jaws of death—these are too often identified with valor, and in the profession of arms such rashness of conduct—what Shakespeare calls, "valor misbegot"—is unjustly applauded; but not so in the Precepts of Knighthood. . . .

> The spiritual aspect of valor is evidenced by composure—calm presence of mind. Tranquility is courage in repose. It is a statical manifestation of valor, as daring deeds are a dynamical. A truly brave man is ever serene; he is never taken by surprise; nothing ruffles the equanimity of his spirit. In the heat of battle he remains cool; in the midst of catastrophes he keeps level his mind. Earthquakes do not shake him, he laughs at storms. We admire him as truly great, who, in the menacing presence of danger or death, retains his self-possession; who, for instance, can compose a poem under impending peril or hum a strain in the face of death.[4]

Courage is doing what you believe is right. Courage that causes action at the wrong time or for the wrong reason is folly. Rash action is to be avoided. Maintaining a serene composure takes courage as well—static courage. Tranquility is courage that rests on the belief that you will do what is right. Courage starts inside of you, in your belief.

Moving from belief to decision to action is the recipe for courage. Courage is a trait that can be learned by anyone willing to take the time to develop it. Courage can compensate for the absence of other deficiencies, as noted by Napoleon at the beginning of the chapter, but courage also has some aspects that can be problematic. When confidence comes from experience, it may come from insufficient experience. When it comes from an ideology, it may cause conflict with others who do not share those beliefs. And, as mentioned several times before, inflated amounts of courage can lead to rash action.

Don't be a *coward*. Be *courageous*, but not so courageous that *you act rashly*. And don't *be ignorant of the consequences*.

Food for Thought

Read this:

1. Read an autobiography of someone you believe is courageous. How does your external opinion of their courage compare against their own opinion of their courage? Where did they put themselves on the scale between too little and too much?

Watch this:

1. In a video internet search engine, type the word *courage*. Choose one of the speakers and hear their version of courage. Do you agree or disagree with the speaker's perspective on the subject? How does it compare to what is written here?

Do this:

1. Roosevelt's recipe for courage requires that you practice facing your fears in a manner that you can plan for until it becomes second nature. Begin today to practice a courageous approach—believe, decide, speak/act—with the little things in your day. Is there a dog that barks at you on your morning run? A pushy friend? Overbearing parents or co-workers? What should you do about it? What will you do to keep your composure, to bear yourself well under trial? Plan ahead. Start small, practice often, grow.
2. Afraid of public speaking? Find a club that lets you face that fear in a safe setting, and overcome it.

References

1. Napoleon Bonaparte, *The Officer's Manual Napoleon's Maxims of War*, trans. Sir George C. D'Aguilar (Richmond, VA: West & Johnson, 1862), 55.

2. Theodore Roosevelt, *An Autobiography by Theodore Roosevelt* (New York: MacMillan Co., 1914), 76.

3. Ibid., 54.

4. Inazo Nitobé, *Bushido: The Soul of Japan* (Tokyo: The Publishing Co., 1909), 25–26.

Conclusion

What do the president of the United States, the captain of the Indian cricket team, a nun, Beyoncé, and my mother all have in common?

They were listed as leaders by a survey participant.

What about Margaret Thatcher, Tom Brady, Vineet Nayar, and Winston Churchill?

Decisive

John F. Kennedy, José Mujica, Khanyi Dlomo, and Martin Luther King, Jr?

Intelligent

The lists go on and on.

Whatever you think leadership looks like, you are one opinion among billions. Defining leadership is a wonderfully elusive task. The definition changes based on where you are, what you are doing, and with whom you are working. The right leader for your efforts won't be the same today as it will be tomorrow. What does that mean? It means that being a leader is a new challenge every day.

There is consistency in leadership. Just like ingredients in your meals, there are traits that combine to make you a leader. Some foods appear on tables all over the world (rice, salt, cheese, fish) and some traits of leadership are universal. These traits are "need to know" and apply to all leadership opportunities. They are the traits listed in this book. Some traits are "nice to know" and vary as widely as the spices that flavor people's meals around the globe. If it is true that variety is the spice of life, then nothing is more exciting than embracing leadership opportunities, doing your best to overcome each challenge, and appreciating the team you have alongside you when you do it.

In this book, you have read writings from the Greek and Roman Empires, the kingdoms of China and Japan, leaders from Africa and the Americas, and many other places. In each case, the authors described or demonstrated key attributes of leaders. Some things never change.

And one truth about leaders remains: **We know one when we see one.**

We do know a leader when we see one, but now decide this: **Are you ready to be one?**

Can you see yourself and your leadership style from the viewpoint of those around you? If not, are you ready to try?

People are already observing you and deciding if you are a leader. Leaders in the survey weren't just members of government, business leaders, or sports champions. There were also people we see in everyday life—nurses, teachers, parents, small business owners, and so on. People are already watching and wondering if you are the leader they need right now where they are.

Marine officers are told that they are leaders because they are officers. Many choose to take that responsibility very seriously and work hard to be a good leader. A few choose to believe they have already made it because of their rank or title, and they do not pursue the traits with sufficient persistence. Which one will you be? Does your title make you a leader, or does your title mean you ought to dedicate time and effort to improving your leadership?

This book focused on the first half of leadership, stemming from this question in the survey:

In your opinion, is leadership a quality you have or something you do?

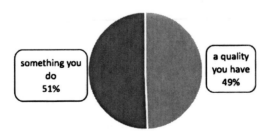

something you do
51%

a quality you have
49%

Leadership is a trait that is the sum of other traits. It is an action that is the sum of daily actions.

The next book will address the primary actions of leadership: What leaders do.

Here are a few final definitions (challenges) from the survey. Is this you? A leader is:

- fair, goal oriented, motivated, motivates and leads those following, supportive, patient, understanding, understands that individuals matter too, knows when to step up and down as leader, and helps others that [they are] leading.
- someone who is willing to bring others to the peak of their lives, someone who inspires, someone who puts others before their self, someone who is passionate about a brighter future, it isn't about telling others what to do with their lives, it's about teaching others about the amazing things they can do with their lives.
- someone who can balance the needs of the organization with the needs of the individuals charged with executing organizational objectives and who can inspire the team to achieve those objectives. A leader must set an example and demonstrate a willingness to do the work required while inspiring others to do it.

Begin training in the traits that make a difference so you're ready when the time comes. It is time to accept the "need to know" traits and practice the steps of each trait, every day. The sooner you start to practice each trait, the sooner they will become a habit.

Good luck. I hope to work with you or for you in the future.

Food for Thought

Read this:

1. Start your reading plan (see chapter on intelligence). Include articles or books about leadership in the rotation. Study it as you would any other subject. Consider taking a leadership course at a local community college, a college,

or university. If your company has a class on management or leadership, take it. Read all the assigned works in that class and use that information to expand your knowledge of "need to know" and "nice to know" traits.

Watch this:
1. As you watch your favorite movies, determine which leadership traits the characters demonstrate. How do you think the character did as a leader? What would you depict differently in the story? What would you do differently?
2. Watch the leaders in your life. What do they do that you admire? Do you admire that trait enough to begin practicing it today? Remember, "imitate, then innovate" is a way to learn a new skill.

Do this:
1. Volunteer for a leadership opportunity today. Coach a youth sports team, plan the company Christmas party, volunteer to manage a fundraiser, whatever. There is *always* an opportunity to volunteer. See it as a leadership training opportunity. Plan and use each of these traits as you manage the opportunity. No matter how it turns out, keep your enthusiasm, review what you learned, and try again. Practice makes perfect, so start practicing today.
2. Find a friend, co-worker, or teammate who also wants to become a leader. Review the traits in this book and honestly identify your strong areas and your areas of weakness. Agree to help each other by pointing out leadership moments in daily situations, moments where you could or should apply one of these traits. Get together regularly to discuss things that have happened to you since you last met and articles or other books you have read on the subject. Encourage one another. Make leadership a subject of conversation, and use it to motivate you to continue to improve. Remember, the Wright brothers pointed out two ways to learn: observe and reflect, or trial and error. They pointed out that trial and error produced the best results. Discussing it is okay, but only if you are also taking on new leadership opportunities whenever you can.
3. Consider the example above, but instead of a teammate, identify a leader you admire and ask them to be a mentor. Specifically mention that you want to improve in the traits of leadership. See where the discussion leads you or ask them to specifically address the "need to know" traits.

Appendix – Online Questionnaire

Today's opinions on leaders and leadership

Survey
verb sur·vey \sər-ˈvā, ˈsər-ˌ\

1
a : to examine as to condition, situation, or value : appraise
b : **to query (someone) in order to collect data for the analysis of some aspect of a group or area**

2
: to determine and delineate the form, extent, and position of (such as a tract of land) by taking linear and angular measurements and by applying the principles of geometry and trigonometry

3
: to view or consider comprehensively

4
: inspect, scrutinize • he surveyed us in a lordly way—Alan Harrington

Crowdsourcing
noun crowd·sourc·ing \ˈkraud-ˌsor-siŋ\
: **the practice of obtaining needed services, ideas, or content by soliciting contributions from a large group of people and especially from the online community rather than from traditional employees or suppliers**

Questionnaire

noun ques·tion·naire \ ˌkwes-chə-ˈner, ˌkwesh-\

1

: a set of questions for obtaining statistically useful or personal information from individuals

2

: a written or printed questionnaire often with spaces for answers

3

: a survey made by the use of a questionnaire

The Questions

While surveys are typically associated with statistical data, the overall objective of this questionnaire was to establish a dialogue with a future readership and include their thoughts within this book. This is more often called crowdsourcing. The results are presented here.

NOTE: If you did not complete the questionnaire when it was originally published, take the survey now. This will allow you to compare your answers with those from around the world. More importantly, it will give you the opportunity to reflect on why you see something one way, while a number of other people may see it another way. Doing the survey "in your mind" or after reading portions of this book will significantly reduce your opportunity to learn from this material.

Define leadership by finishing the following sentence: "A leader is . . ."

_____

_____

_____

Name one person (past or present) that you think of when you hear the word "leader":

_____

In one word, what is the primary role, job title, or position of the person you named in the previous question?

_____

For the person you named, what one trait do you believe most strongly contributes to your opinion of them as a leader? Please use one word to complete the following sentence: "He or she is very. . ."

_____

For the person you named, what do they do differently that makes them a leader? Please complete the following sentence: "I especially notice the way this person. . ."

_____

Do you hope to be like this person?
- ☐ Yes
- ☐ No

In your opinion, is leadership a quality you have or something you do?
- ☐ a quality you have
- ☐ something you do

Is leadership something that you are born with, or something you can learn?
- ☐ something you're born with
- ☐ something you can learn

What is your country of origin?

_____

What is your gender?
- ☐ Male
- ☐ Female
- ☐ Other

What is your age?

- [ ] <18
- [ ] 18–25
- [ ] 26–35
- [ ] 36–45
- [ ] 46–55
- [ ] 56–65
- [ ] >65

Data Scrubbing

The survey was left open for one month and was advertised through academic channels, multiple forms of digital media, professional organizations, and word of mouth. A total of 529 entries were recorded. Four entries were discarded, one for incompleteness and three for plagiarism (responses were perfectly identical, so copies were discarded). The remaining 525 were normalized ("scrubbed") in the manner expressed here. These corrections were necessary due to the open form of the questions as well as the requirement to use English, which was a second language for many participants. These factors compounded to allow for user preferred spellings, misspellings, foreign keyboard symbols, and so forth. Objective and subjective corrections were made to the data, as described below, to put "like with like" and better learn from the results of the questionnaire.

Objective Corrections

Objective corrections are those that correct grammar and spelling or put similar answers together in the English language. If interpreted, the data are understood in such a way that I believed most people would conclude the same on their own or agree with the chosen interpretation. Examples include removing capital letters from the traits to group them with each other or correcting misspelled words. Also, I removed spaces that were found at the end of some entries, which are commonly inserted when selecting a word from a spell-predict program (common on cell phones). For example, "Canada " = "Canada." These spaces prevented the grouping of data. The other objective corrections are listed here.

Name one person (past or present) that you think of when you hear the word "leader":

Gandhi = Mahatma Gandhi
Churchill = Winston Churchill
Alexander = Alexander the Great = Alexander the great = **Alexander the Great**
Barack Obama, Barak Obama, President Barack Obama, Obama, President
    Obama = **Barack Obama**
Martin Luther King, MLK, Martin Luther King, Jr. Dr. Martin Luther King, Jr.
    = **Martin Luther King, Jr.**

In one word, what is the primary role, job title, or position of the person you named in the previous question?

President, former president, POTUS, former POTUS, retired president, president formerly = **President**

Dad, my dad, father = **Father**

Mother, my mother (NOTE: names were deleted; i.e., "my mother Jane Doe") = **Mother**

Chancellor of Germany, federal chancellor, Bundeskanzlerin = **Chancellor of Germany**

For the person you named, what one trait do you believe most strongly contributes to your opinion of them as a leader? Please use one word to complete the following sentence: "He or she is very. . . "

Vision, visionary, a visionary	= **visionary**
Integrity, has integrity	= **integrity**
Action driven, action oriented	= **action-oriented**
Articulate, articulated, good communicator, good at communicating	= **articulate**
Calculated, calculating	= **calculating**
Charismatic, charism, Charisma, charisma, Carismatico	= **charismatic**
Compassionate, compassion	= **compassionate**

For the person you named, what do they do differently that makes them a leader? Please complete the following sentence: "I especially notice the way this person. . ."

No corrections were made to this section, which will be the primary topic of Book II.

What is your country of origin?

America, American!, American, The united states, United States, united states of America, United States of America, US of A, U.S.A., America!!! = **USA**

Britain, England, UK	=UK
INDIA, India, Indian	= India
Jamaica, jamaica, Jamaica BOOM!	= Jamaica
China, Chinese	= China
Russian Federation	= Russia
Peru, peru, Perú	= Peru

Subjective Corrections

Subjective corrections are those that were interpreted in a way that changed the data entry but that I believed would be accepted by a majority of readers. These decisions were necessary to collect the data together for grouping/counting. An example is removing titles from the names, since the title was also given in the question that asked for the "role, title, or position." This avoided duplication of some data and allowed data management programs to group entries. Example: President Barack Obama is Barack Obama in the role of President. The data are present but organized to allow all versions of the name to be collected together. The other subjective corrections are listed here.

All instances of "former" and "ex" were removed. Example: former president, ex-president = "President"

For persons who were listed in various roles, the role occurring most often was kept. Example, Colin Powell was the Secretary of State, Chairman of the Joint Chiefs of Staff (CJCS), and a General. CJCS was most common and was therefore kept as the role for Colin Powell.

For persons in the role of CEO, several were also listed "CEO and founder." Those who were CEO and founder (i.e., Jack Ma, Elon Musk, Steve Jobs) were given the title of "CEO and founder." Those who were CEOs of companies they did not create (i.e., Jack Welch) were listed as "CEO."

Napoleon Bonaparte was listed as emperor and a general in equal number. "Emperor, general" was used.

All personages who founded a religion were listed as "religious founders," although many other titles were offered.

(For Dr. Martin Luther King, Jr.) Civil Rights Activist, Civil Rights Leader, Civil Rights Movement Activist, Minister = **Civil Rights movement leader**

(For Gandhi) freedom fighter, revolutionary, representative, barrister, pacifist, activist, leader of the independence movement, Led India to independence from British rule, Influence the people toward the main goals, advocator   = **Independence leader**

(For Nelson Mandela) Activist, Advocate, ANC former leader, Anti-apartheidsstrijder, apartheid, Former president of South Africa, guide, Head of State, Inspire, Movement leader, Political opponent,
    Politician, president, President of South Africa, Referent, Statesman, Visionary, world leader   = **President of South Africa**
    If multiple traits were listed as an answer, the first trait was kept.

Some traits were grouped together:

Egoless = unselfish = selfless
Intelligent = intellectual = intelligence
Modest = humble
No lies = honest
Open to new ideas = open-minded = open
Innovative = creative
Persevering = persistent
Orator = eloquent
Listened = attentive

Where some participants used phrases to describe a trait, their phrase was reduced to a single word that I believed best represented their intent:

Care with its employees = caring

consequent in his believes = dedicated

Desire to make America great again. Business acumen. He is very clear about what he wants to achieve = focused

Does not let anybody do anything other than what he wants = controlling

good at resolving conflicts bringing clarity and direction to the team = teambuilder

good at surrounding himself with people who are experts in their field to make better-informed decisions = teambuilder

He keeps everyone in picture and arranged weekly meetings to discuss the progress = communicative

He treats people well = considerate

He walked away from power = humble

Reference to a human rights movement = dedicated

Scope of Impact = influential

Thinker = pensive

This individual was able to listen to dissenting views and obtain consensus = attentive through as he managed to conquer nearly all of Asia = thorough

Results

The opinions expressed in this survey could reinforce or challenge some ideas that you have about leaders and leadership. The data below are presented in a neutral manner to avoid introducing additional conclusions at this point in the book. Relevant analysis is included in the text of the book. The definitions of leadership, 525 of them, are not presented here for consideration of space, but many of them are utilized throughout the book.

Confidence springs from our perception of ourselves, but effectiveness as a leader springs from the perceptions that others have about us. The information below gives you an opportunity to see what others think about leaders and, therefore, gives you an insight into how others may perceive you as a leader and/or your leadership potential. Read the following information, see it from a neutral point of view, and ask yourself the following questions:

1. Do people see these traits in me? Which ones? How do I exhibit them? When?
2. Are there people on this list I do not know? What can I learn about them?
3. What traits do I most admire?

*Name one person (past or present) that you think of when you hear the word "leader":
Listed in order of mentions in the questionnaire. Read—Left column first, top to
bottom. After that, the 20 persons with the most mentions in the survey are listed,
along with the number of countries with participants who mentioned them.*

Barack Obama	Carlos Ghosn	Recep Tayyip Erdoğan
Nelson Mandela	Theodore Roosevelt	Erich M.
Martin Luther King, Jr.	Franklin D. Roosevelt	Spartacus
Mahatma Gandhi	Dalai Lama	Ernest Shackleton
Winston Churchill	Oprah Winfrey	Tiago Patel
Jesus Christ	Joe Dunford	Ernie Hughes
My mother	Myself	Denys
Steve Jobs	Dale Carnegie	Father John
George Washington	Genghis Khan	Xi Jingping
Adolf Hitler	James Mattis	Fatima
Richard Branson	Norman Schwarzkopf	Charles Puyol
Angela Merkel	Beyoncé	Felix Houphouet Boigny
Ronald Reagan	Alexander the Great	Col Art C., USMC
Narendra Modi	My former manager	Former boss
Abraham Lincoln	Ellen	Paul Keating
Donald Trump	Colin Powell	Former restaurant man-
Jack Welch	Muhammad Ali Jinnah	ager
Francis	My boss	Craig Jelinek
My father	John Paul II	Admiral Mike Rogers
Mother Teresa	Zulfiqar Ali Bhutto	Rodrigo M.
A P J Abdul Kalam	Vladimir Putin	Frank Dunn
Elon Musk	Mustafa Kemal Atatürk	Sheila Fraser
Bill Gates	Téa Leoni	Barbara H.
Napoleon Bonaparte	Ari Uusikartano	Steven Gerrard
John F. Kennedy	My parents	Gary
Bernie Sanders	Dr. Cassity	The queen
Prophet Muhammad	Santosh K.	Gary Vaynerchuk
Michelle Obama	Dwight Eisenhower	Torben
Thabo Mbeki	Vaidyanathan	Gautama Buddha
Jack Ma	El Gran Capitan	Vladimir Komarov
José Mourinho	My English teacher	Gen(ret) Blaine Holt
George Patton	Audie Murphy	Mr. Schweitzer
Mahender Singh Dhoni	CDR Peter R.	Batman
Che Guevara	Bala	my best friend

Benjamin Franklin
My cousin
A teacher
My former boss
Harriet Tubman
My last skipper
Hassan
Chester W. Nimitz
Henry Ford
Nicole D.
Hornblower
Company president
Houari Boumédiène
Peter Thiel
Hunter O.
George W. Bush
Ian Sharp
Rafael Nadal
Indi (a previous boss)
Richard D. Winters
Jack B.
Sachin Tendulkar
Albert Einstein
school principal
Bhagat Singh
Simon Sinek
Jacques Chirac
Andy Meier
Jamal
Subodh T.
Bill Belichek
Adina
Javier Mascherano
Thomas C.
Javion
Tom Brady
Jawaharlal Nehru
Tshidi M.
Jean-Marc P.

Vikram C.
Jeff Immelt
Wayne State SOM's
president
Jeffery R Holland
Mr. A
Jerry Nutter
Cathy L.
Achraf Rifi
My adviser in college
Joan of Arc
Brian Clough
My classmate
Johan Larsson
My current manager
Bruce
Charles de Gaulle
John F. Kennedy
My former manager
Cael Sanderson
My husband
Jonathan T.
Ana Lucia
Caesar (Julius)
My past SVP
Jose Mujica
COL (R) Howie C.
José Mujica
Andres O.
José N. T.
No one
Judah K.
Olof Palme
Kartik Sharma
Past boss Brian
Khanyi Dlomo
Kim Jong Un
Pope
King Willem-

Alexander
Pravin Gordhan
KMH
Prince Sidon (Legend
of Zelda)
CAPT Mark Bailey
Qin Shi Huang
Ray Mehringer
Lewis and Clarke
Dad
Louwke VDS
Rodrigo Diaz de Vivar
El Cid
Carlos
Dag Hammarskjöld
Alin Burcea
Sadiq Khan
Mahendra Singh Dhoni
Sara P.
Sheikh Zayed
Malala Yousafzi
Sheryl Sandberg
Mao Zhe Dong
Soraya Tarzi
Marcelo Rebelo de Sousa
Stan McChrystal
Marcus Garvey
Steve R.
Margaret Thatcher
Subhas Chandra Bose
Mark P.
Taiichi Ohno
Mark Zuckerberg
Tenzin Gyatso
Carlos Goshn
The Pope
Mary Wall
Dave Robson
Matthiew

What Leaders Are

Thomas Sanders   Tristan Tzara   Mitch
Michael Jordan   Michele Fluornoy   Warren Buffet
Tim Cook   Umar farooq (RA)   Monika Liikamaa
Michael Schumacher   Valery Lobanovsky   William Wallace
Tom S.   Mike Ditka   Konrad Adenauer
Micheal Bloomberg   Vineet Nayar   Laverne Cox

Name one person (past or present) that you think of when you hear the word "leader":	# of countries which included at least one vote for this person
Barack Obama	25
Nelson Mandela	22
Martin Luther King, Jr.	13
Mahatma Gandhi	12
Winston Churchill	8
Jesus Christ	4
My mother	6
Steve Jobs	9
George Washington	1
Adolf Hitler	6
Richard Branson	7
Angela Merkel	6
Ronald Reagan	1
Narendra Modi	1
Abraham Lincoln	4
Donald Trump	2
Jack Welch	4
Francis	5
My father	4
Mother Teresa	4

In one word, what is the primary role, job title, or position of the person you named in the previous question? Read—Left column first, top to bottom.

US President
President of South Africa
Civil Rights Movement
CEO and founder
CEO
Independence leader
Chancellor of Germany
Religious Founder
Prime Minister of UK
Religious Leader
Prime Minister of India
Revolutionary
General
Captain, Indian Cricket Team
Project Manager
Manager
Soccer Coach
Nun
Emperor, general
Mother
FLOTUS
King
CIO
President of India
Commander
US Senator
President of France
Lecturer
Secretary of Defense
CJCS
Admiral
COO
Prime Minister of Pakistan
Director

Leader of the Mongol clans
Activist
Media personality
Actor
Founder of Pakistan
President of Uruguay
Artist
Principal
General
Guide
Teacher
President
Business Owner
Prime Minister of Australia
El Rey (The King)
Soldier
Client engagement
President of Portugal
Republic
Engineer
Professor
Entrepreneur
Parent
Entrepreneur
DA
President of Turkey
Executive Business Manager
Prime minister of Sweden
Explorer
F1 driver
Retired

Finance and Operation Director, my mentor
Self-employed
First Emperor of Qin dynasty
Strategist
Coach
Poet
Football Coach
President of China
Footballer
CFO
Chairman
President of Russia
Founder of Turkey
Dad
Freedom Fighter
Author
Prince
Purchasing manager
Commander Royal Navy
Release Train Engineer
Commanding Officer
Researcher
General Manager
Roman general
Good Cricketer
Class rep
Commodore
Actress
Squadron Commander
Director of nursing
Head BI Competence Center
Planner
Head coach

Portfolio Manager
Head of department
President of Algeria
Head of the administration
President of company
HR
President of I.P. Sharp Associates Ltd.
HR
President of Ivory Coast
Husband
President of programming and operations, fraud Analyst
Associate Director
Auditor General of Canada
IT
President of UAE
Actress and Activist for women and children
Priest
Lead programmer
Prime Minister of England

Charge Nurse in the ER
Dalai Lama
Class rep
Bcio
Coordinator
Dean of Students
Wayne State President
Blogger
Quarterback
Queen
Mayor of New York
Boss
Cosmonaut
Research University
Middle manager
Supervisor
Caliph
Teacher
Sales Director
Tennis Player
Scientist
Undersecretary of Defense for Policy
Senior Engineer
Country head
Soccer Team Captain

Sport star
Nail Technician
Statesman
NCO
Student
Creator of Toyota Manufacturing System
Parent
Minister of Finance
Team Leader
US Marine
UN Secretary General
US Rep to NATO
University President
My first boss
My old manager
Captain
Visionary
CEO of HCL Technologies
My father
Captain of Liverpool FC
Mother
Managing Director
Mayor of London

For the person you named, what one trait do you believe most strongly contributes to your opinion of them as a leader? Please use one word to complete the following sentence: "He or she is very. . ." Read—Left column first, top to bottom.

inspirational	articulate	followable
charismatic	respectful	honorable
visionary	responsible	composed
humble	helpful	pragmatic
strong	strong willed	strategic
persistent	encouraging	principled
compassionate	conscientious	knowledgeable
selfless	commanding	controlling
determined	straightforward	farsighted
courageous	dynamic	inclusive
intelligent	focused	thorough
passionate	people oriented	convincing
decisive	results oriented	organized
driven	effective	action oriented
wise	involved	forthright
caring	eloquent	righteous
dedicated	kind	genuine
confident	powerful	service-
honest	supportive	oriented
committed	resilient	proactive
smart	trustworthy	avant-garde
thoughtful	innovative	respectable
influential	bold	good listener
open-minded	hardworking	compelling
motivational	ethical	affinity
patient	coherent	witty
calm	successful	aggressiveness
authentic	aware	receptive
persuasive	competent	convinced
empathetic	disciplined	endearing
brave	fair	calculating
creative	ambitious	staunch
attentive	team player	human
consistent	positive	famous

What Leaders Are

humanitarian
advisor
cool
present
aligned with values
progressive
accepting of risk
reliable
accepting
empowering
cheerful
engaging
demanding
skillful
integrity
stoical
experimented
intrepid
intuitive
firm
inventive
believable
democratic socialist

freedom
detailed
embracing
clear
focused
real
likable
relentless
logical
emotional intelligent
loving
communicative
megalomaniac
authoritative
motivating
rooted
devoted
servant
observant
sincere
dignified
enlightened
dignifying

steadfast
outgoing
enlightened
direct
exceptional
astute
auto-determination
peacemaker
talented
pensive
team-builder
dishonest
tenacious
collaborative
flexible
personable
understanding
combative
considerate
eclectic
active
adept

Five most commonly named leaders, with traits listed in order of the most frequently named to least frequently named:

Barack Obama	Nelson Mandela	Martin Luther King, Jr.	Mahatma Gandhi	Winston Churchill
charismatic	inspirational	inspirational	strong	persistent
inspirational	strong	charismatic	inspirational	wise
humble	selfless	persistent	courageous	strong
calm	persistent	articulate	determined	confident
strong	dedicated	consistent	rooted	open-minded
authentic	visionary	selfless	kind	decisive
persistent	passionate	respectful	trustworthy	resilient
empathetic	humble	passionate	auto-determination	eloquent
smart	resilient	intelligent	patient	visionary
observant	focused	committed	wise	intelligent
progressive	straightforward	courageous	charismatic	committed
persuasive	attentive	freedom	aligned with values	involved
dignifying	courageous	caring	coherent	
likable	compassionate	determined	believable	
driven	combative	forthright	humble	
passionate	open-minded			
embracing	exceptional			
principled	consistent			
caring	genuine			
kind	people oriented			
followable				
motivational				
honorable				
open-minded				
commanding				
confident				
respectful				
present				
competent				
problem-focused				
thoughtful				
dignified				
composed				
influential				
team builder				
innovative				
visionary				
articulate				
intelligent				

For the person you named, what do they do differently that makes them a leader? Please complete the following sentence: "I especially notice the way this person. . ."

Like the definitions, these are not reprinted here due to space. These will be the subject of another book—*What Leaders Do.*

(For the person you named) Do you hope to be like this person?

Do you hope to be like the person you named as a leader?

In your opinion, is leadership a quality you have or something you do?

In your opinion, is leadership a quality you have or something you do?

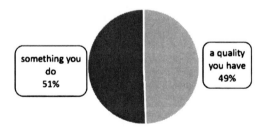

Is leadership something that you are born with, or something you can learn?

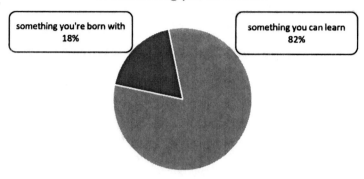

What is your country of origin? (listed alphabetically)

Afghanistan	Hungary	Pakistan
Algeria	India	Peru
Angola	Indonesia	Philippines
Australia	Iraq	Poland
Austria	Ireland	Portugal
Bangladesh	Italy	Romania
Barbados	Ivory Coast	Russia
Belarus	Jamaica	Singapore
Brazil	Japan	South Africa
Canada	Jordan	South Korea
China	Kosovo	Spain
Colombia	Kyrgyztan	Sweden
Cyprus	Latvia	Switzerland
Denmark	Lebanon	Taiwan
Ecuador	Malaysia	Trinidad and Tobago
Egypt	Malta	Tunisia
El Salvador	Mexico	Turkey
Finland	Monaco	UK
France	Morocco	Ukraine
Germany	Netherlands	USA
Ghana	New Zealand	Venezuela
Greece	Nigeria	Yemen
Guatemala	Norway	

What is your gender?

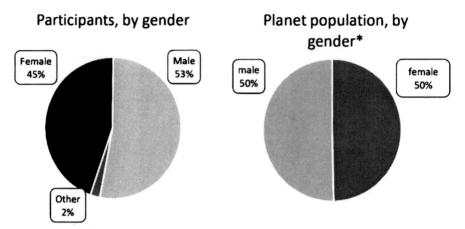

What is your age? (NOTE: the age distribution of the participants is not equal to that of the population.)

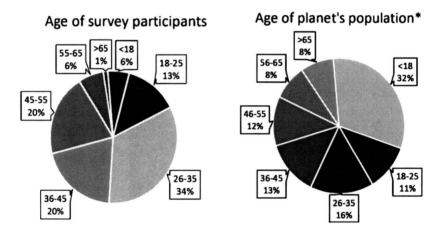

*United States Census Bureau, Demographic Internet Staff. "International Programs, International Data Base." World Population by Age and Sex—US Census Bureau. June 27, 2011. Accessed May 4, 2017. https://www.census.gov/population/international/data/idb/worldpop.php.

Acknowledgments

In order to live up to my own standards for leadership, I must appreciate the people who were part of the process of turning an idea into a manuscript and, eventually, a published book.

My classmates in the EDHEC MBA helped plant the seed for this idea. So many of us were eager to further our management and leadership skills but found that the leadership portion of the syllabus was just the beginning of the process. The discussions that took place after class required me to consider a more conversable and concrete structure for discussing the subject. There was an evident need to discuss leadership as a more concrete topic.

My first thanks must go to Dr. Michelle Sisto, director of the EDHEC Global MBA, who allowed me to select this as a topic for a thesis, and to my faculty advisor, Dr. Declan Murphy, who worked with me to shape the direction of the text and move it forward into a form that was acceptable as an academic submission.

After the academic requirement was met, I was assisted by Melissa Stewart, a journalist who helped transform an academic assignment into the more readable and articulate format of this book. The many recommendations that she offered became part of the manuscript submitted to Lucid Books. There, the publishing team came alongside and, with their knowledge and experience, turned the idea into a product that was professional in both presentation and attitude. I have learned a lot from Melissa's reviews and from the editing and publishing teams at Lucid Books. If you have never written a book, believe me when I say it will be an educational process. I highly recommend it.

Leadership can be a dry topic, as evidenced by the academic version of my manuscript. For this reason, I especially appreciate my wife taking the time to read the manuscript after the draft was complete.

To the reader, thank you for spending your time with me in the pages of this book. I hope it meets or exceeds your expectations.

About the Author

Nathan Neblett served for 24 years as an officer of the United States Marine Corps, during which time he observed leaders as they oversaw units comprising between 2 and 25,000 people across the four military branches and the United States Coast Guard. He was assigned as a liaison and advisor to foreign militaries in Asia, the Middle East, and Europe, and worked with military personnel from Central and South America. Additionally, he served at a US Embassy, working alongside the US Department of State.

Nathan has been a pilot, instructor pilot, test pilot, teacher, soccer coach, foreign area officer, and a father. He has led flight crews, project teams, classrooms, soccer teams, detachments, offices, and his family (along with his wife, who has done the lioness's share of the work).

Nathan's education includes a BS in Aerospace Engineering from the US Naval Academy, an MS in Aviation Systems from the University of Tennessee, an MA in Government and International Relations from Regent University, and an MBA at the École des Hautes Études Commerciales (EDHEC) in Nice, France. He has also completed various military education programs.

His failures, as much as his successes, created his desire to share what he has learned. He hopes to help others succeed as leaders in their careers and lives.

CPSIA information can be obtained
at www.ICGtesting.com
Printed in the USA
FFOW01n0939230518
46772171-48945FF